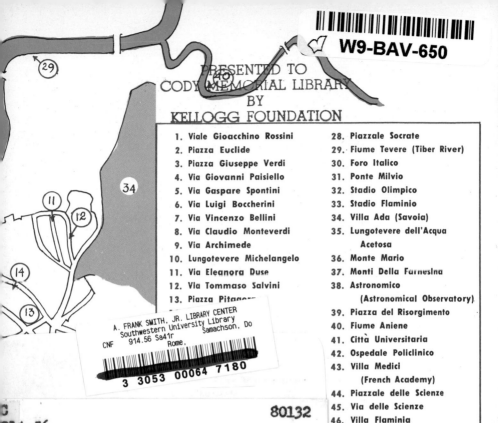

1. Viale Gioacchino Rossini
2. Piazza Euclide
3. Piazza Giuseppe Verdi
4. Via Giovanni Paisiello
5. Via Gaspare Spontini
6. Via Luigi Boccherini
7. Via Vincenzo Bellini
8. Via Claudio Monteverdi
9. Via Archimede
10. Lungotevere Michelangelo
11. Via Eleanora Duse
12. Via Tommaso Salvini
13. Piazza Pitagora

28. Piazzale Socrate
29. Fiume Tevere (Tiber River)
30. Foro Italico
31. Ponte Milvio
32. Stadio Olimpico
33. Stadio Flaminio
34. Villa Ada (Savoia)
35. Lungotevere dell'Acqua
    Acetosa
36. Monte Mario
37. Monti Della Farnesina
38. Astronomico
    (Astronomical Observatory)
39. Piazza del Risorgimento
40. Fiume Aniene
41. Città Universitaria
42. Ospedale Policlinico
43. Villa Medici
    (French Academy)
44. Piazzale delle Scienze
45. Via delle Scienze
46. Villa Flaminia
47. Monte Gianicolo
48. Città del Vaticano
49. Villa Borghese
50. Pincio
51. Parioli
no (Cemetery)

ROME

*St. Peter's Square and
Basilica, at the end of
Via della Conciliazione*

CITIES
of the
WORLD

ROME

By DOROTHY and JOSEPH SAMACHSON

Illustrated by EMIL WEISS

80132

Rand McNally & Company

Chicago · New York · San Francisco

To Professore Gianfranco Mazzuoli,
whose kindness and hospitality
contributed so greatly to our
pleasure in knowing Rome.

CONTENTS

ILLUSTRATIONS

MAPS

I.

THE EVER-CHANGING
ETERNAL CITY

For centuries it has been proverbial that all roads lead to Rome. Two thousand years ago, returning conquerors drove their prisoners to the capital of the Roman Empire along the great highways, or brought them up to the mouth of the Fiume Tevere (River Tiber) by ship. In the Middle Ages, pilgrims from all over Europe sought the city that was the fountainhead of their religion. And ever since the eighteenth century, hundreds of thousands of visitors have made the journey—on foot, on horseback, and in carriages and, in our own day, by plane, railroad, automobile, or motorcycle.

It is a fascinating sight to drive along the highway and see a cross section of those who are traveling toward Rome on motorbikes and motorcycles: a young husband, wife, and child; a friar in a brown robe, who seems to have stepped out of a picture of the Middle Ages; a young man and a girl; a pair of young men; a middle-aged couple.

Rome has always had something for everyone. Above it are the sunny skies that have long lured the Englishman, tired of his native rain; and on its soil are the splendors of sculpture and architecture that attract the Japanese tourist seeking a change from the simple dignity of his own country's masterpieces.

Rome was probably founded in 753 B.C. Little survives from this very early period, for the city was captured and burned by the Gauls in 390 B.C. It was completely rebuilt after the Gauls left, and grand and imposing edifices were added as Rome grew, to become the capital, first of Italy, and then of the civilized Western World.

The ability of its people to pick up their city from the ruins of fire and conquest and make it flourish more brilliantly than ever has earned it the proud designation of the Eternal City. The name, however, is misleading, for the village that thrived on violence more than seven hundred years before the birth of Christ was quite different from the imperial city of the Caesars, from the medieval Rome that became the center of the Christian world, and from the bustling Rome of today. As Venice may be called a City of Canals, Rome may be called— among many other things—a City of Fountains. The fountains while not, perhaps, eternal, do not change from year to year, although the water that gives them life is never the same from second to second. Rome is also a City of Cats and, like its feline inhabitants, has had many lives.

Remains of all the cities of the past survive in the city of the present and are one of its most remarkable features. Even the ancient myths seem to come to life as one walks through Rome. In the center of the city, next to the

Campidoglio, or Capitol, is a cage containing a she-wolf (sometimes with a companion), a living symbol of the wolf which, according to legend, nursed the infants Romulus and Remus (Romolo and Remo). When the twins were grown, in a quarrel, Romulus killed Remus, then went on to found Rome himself and become its first king. Temples to the old Roman gods are everywhere, and new buildings stand in the old Campo Marzio or Campus Martius (Field of Mars)—the God of War and, supposedly, the father of Romulus and Remus. On the outskirts of the city can be found a Temple of Romulus, and a Temple of the Nymph (Tempio Ninfa) Egeria, who married the legendary second king, Numa Pompilius (Pompilio).

Both temples are near the Via Appia Antica (Old Appian Way), a road that has

Fountain of Rivers (Fontana dei Fiumi)

11

Old Appian Way

Roman Forum

survived for almost twenty-three centuries and is still in use. Less than a mile apart are the Tomb of the Scipione—generals who led Rome to victory against the rival empire of Carthage—and a church named Domine, Quo Vadis? to mark the spot where Saint Peter, after the Crucifixion, saw the image of Christ and said, *"Domine, Quo Vadis?"* ("Oh, Lord, where goest Thou?").

The old Foro Romano (Roman Forum), where the people of an expanding city met to talk, to bargain in the marketplace, and to listen to public speakers, has given its name to discussion groups in the modern world. Close by the Forum is the Colosseo (Colosseum) built by slave labor, where gladiators fought in deadly combat and the early Christians were thrown to wild beasts. Streets, buildings, and columns keep alive the memories of the different emperors. One can find a street named for Julius Caesar (Giulio Cesare), who first seized absolute power, although he was never emperor in name, along with the Foro di Augusto (Augustus), Mausoleo d'Adriano (Tomb of Hadrian), Terme di Diocleziano (Baths of Diocletian), the Baths of Caracalla, and other monuments to long-dead rulers.

It is essentially in the churches that the ancient, the medieval, and the modern mingle with the most striking effect. The Basilica di San Pietro (Saint Peter's Basilica), one of the landmarks of Rome, was started in the middle of the fifteenth century on the site of the Basilica of Constantine, which itself dated back to the year 324 A.D. (see Frontispiece). Other churches are often built on the sites of older basilicas or even on the sites of pagan temples. Objects inside the churches are also usually a combination of ancient and modern.

During the past two decades, Rome has been given a new name—City of Illusion. It has been the setting for many movies, such as *Open City, Roman Holiday,* and *Three Coins in the Fountain,* which centers about the Fontana di Trevi (Fountain of Trevi). The movie, whose plot was based on the superstition that coins thrown into the fountain would help ensure the visitor's return, has influenced the habits of tourists so greatly that some toss coins into all sorts of fountains, including those of churches.

For almost two thousand years Rome has hidden a City of the Dead. Beneath the surface of Rome and its outskirts

*A visitor tossing a coin into the water of the
Fountain of Trevi*

In the catacombs

are the Catacombe, which consist of miles of underground tunnels cut out of the soft Roman rock on as
many as five different levels. These tunnels were used to
provide burial places for the early Christians and, as the
religous persecution of Christians increased, they began to
serve also as places of worship. It is estimated that a hundred thousand bodies were entombed in the Catacombs,
whose gloomy tunnels remain cool even during the hottest
days of the Roman summer.

Rome is situated in the middle of a rolling plain on
what is mostly volcanic soil. It was known early in its
history for its Seven Hills, but the modern city has added
new hills to the original seven. A walk in the city therefore has its conspicuous ups and downs, from about forty
feet above sea level to four hundred and fifty feet above
on Monte Mario. This hill on the right side of the Tiber
houses the Istituto Astronomico (Astronomical Institute

or Observatory), and offers a magnificent panoramic view of the city.

The Roman climate is often thought of as semitropical, and such trees as palms and cypresses, figs, olives, and oleanders abound. But Rome is, in fact, farther north than such a Temperate Zone city as New York, the latitude of Rome being 41° 53′ N, while the latitude of New York is only 40° 21′ N. Rome, like the entire Italian peninsula, is protected from north winds by the Alps, and the surrounding seas help keep the summer temperature down. The average winter temperature is about 45° Fahrenheit, and during the summer about 80°. It is not surprising, therefore, to find that pines are more common than palms, and are in fact so characteristic of Rome and so beloved that the composer Otterino Respighi wrote a symphonic composition called *The Pines of Rome*. The summer is generally dry, although the air may be humid, and the rest of the year is no more than reasonably rainy, the total rainfall averaging only thirty-two inches.

At the time of the Emperors, the population of Rome is supposed to have reached two million. As the city suffered from invasion, fire, and plague, however, the population declined to a low of about 80,000 during the Middle Ages. It stayed at approximately this level for centuries. Then, with the unification of Italy under a single government, the population began to grow rapidly again. From 1870 on, it more than doubled every thirty years, and the 200,000 inhabitants of that year have been replaced by ten times that number of modern Romans, at least as many as lived during the great days of the ancient city.

Many of these are former peasants or the children of peasants, and a number of peasant customs still survive. Occasionally, for instance, one sees a woman walking along with a basket balanced on her head, as was common in the old days. But she usually returns to her home outside the city after she has sold her eggs or vegetables at one of the many outdoor markets. Peasant customs do not penetrate the Via Veneto, the street that is the center of elegant night clubs and sidewalk restaurants.

Peasant women, carrying baskets to market

As a result of the growth of population, of bombardment, and in some cases of the desire to replace old and no longer useful buildings by new ones, there has been considerable construction, and the face of the city as a whole has changed much during the past century. Some parks and villas have given way to new business and apartment buildings. But the history of Rome stands in the way of architectural planning. Sometimes dilapidated buildings are torn down to make way for

Outdoor fruit market

Modern architecture—a new hotel

modern structures, only to reveal at their foundations ruins of the ancient city. At this point the government steps in and forbids destruction of the ruins, and those archaeologists who are not busy elsewhere take over.

This is what occurred in the Largo di Torre Argentina (Argentina Tower Square), not far from the center of Rome. An entire block of temple ruins was uncovered, and the plans for new apartment houses had to be abandoned. The old ruins did not go uninhabited, however. Gradually, the cats of Rome moved in, and now the square is the unofficial headquarters for cats, who live and fight there by the hundreds, dozing in the shade of the ruins during the day, coming out hungrily to eat the food that

18

visitors throw them, and reviving fully only at night. Fortunately, there is very little caterwauling. In Rome, cats and people get along nicely together.

Because of the obligation to leave the ruins untouched, many of the modern buildings have been constructed on the outskirts of Rome. Meanwhile, the center of the city remains a fascinating and confusing mixture of ancient, medieval, and modern, the last being amply represented by the compact automobiles and motorcycles with which the city abounds.

Traffic laws permit more than they forbid, and at times it appears that the people of Rome are all playing a mad game in which they risk their lives every time they

A traffic jam in Piazza Barberini

cross a street. But the danger is not quite as great as it seems. Drivers do keep an eye out for the pedestrian, although they do not like to stop for one. They swerve to right or left, slowing down little, if any, and if the pedestrian keeps his nerve, all is well.

Visitors prefer to tackle traffic where the crossings are plainly marked,

Traffic policemen and especially where a policeman can act as referee, but native Romans are

more casual, and cross anywhere. In many places, of course, the visitor has no choice but to do as the Romans do, for some of the streets have sidewalks too narrow to permit passage in two directions at once, and others have no sidewalks at all. Here the vehicles and pedestrians pick their way past each other, between rows of buildings, like ants and beetles crawling competitively through a tunnel.

It is the old streets that are most constricted. However, Rome also has its share of wide avenues and broad

A narrow street in Trastevere

20

A wide street—Via Veneto

sidewalks where walking offers little difficulty other than that of getting past the sidewalk restaurants without sitting down for anything from a bottle of wine to a dish of ice cream. (The frequent "bars" serve coffee, milk products, and soft drinks as well as alcoholic drinks.)

There *is* a psychological difficulty—that of passing the streets without stopping to wonder at their names. For the streets and squares and bridges of Rome reflect not only the history of the city and the country, but the history of the world. You will find a Via Garibaldi, a Piazzale Garibaldi (esplanade), and a Ponte Garibaldi (bridge), a Cavour Street, a Piazza Vittorio Emanuele (Victor Emmanuel Square), a Cola di Rienzo Street and Square, and many other names that honor the heroes of Italian history, along with a Giorgio Washington Avenue named for the father of our own country, and a Bolivar Square, for the

21

Washington of South America. Via Americo Vespucci recalls the geographer who gave his name to a hemisphere. Via Ferdinando Gregorovius honors a historian of Rome itself. Events of the past are likewise recalled, as on the Gianicolo, or Janiculum Hill, where the walks are adorned with busts representing the patriots who fought with Garibaldi, protected by his statue on a horse, and in the Parco della Rimembranza (Park of Remembrance) where every living tree is said to represent a dead soldier.

You can find in Rome both a Via and a Piazzale delle Scienze, and such places as Via Fermi and Piazza Fermi, in honor of the Italian physicist, and Via Alberto Einstein, in honor of a German physicist, both Nobel Prize winners who became American citizens; Via Galvani, Via Volta, Via Galilei, Piazza Euclide, Piazza Pitagora (Pythagoras), Via Archimede, and Piazzale Socrate, named for great physicists, mathematicians, and a philosopher. Viale Da Vinci and Lungotevere (Street along the Tiber) Michelangelo give painting and sculpture part of their due. Via Eleanora Duse and Via Tommaso Salvini recall a great actress and actor. Places named Piazza Giuseppe Verdi, Viale Gioacchino Rossini, Via Paisiello, and others pay tribute to music. Sometimes, even if a great man was on the losing side of a battle, he still receives honor. Via Giordano Bruno, for example, is named for the philosopher who was imprisoned and burned by the Inquisition.

If the arts and sciences have their due, religion can hardly be called neglected. The places named for saints and holy events seem endless and, to round out the picture of human life, there is not only a Via dell'Acquasanta

(Street of the Holy Water) but also a Lungotevere Acqua Acetosa (Street along the Tiber of the Vinegary Water)!

If the number of street names seems far to exceed the number of streets, this is because many streets change their names every few blocks. Sometimes they broaden into a square, and this will have its own name. The Romans have always found places to name after a great man, woman, or event.

Despite its more than eight thousand street names, Rome is not a large city. Its perimeter is less than fifteen miles, and, in any direction, one side of the city is no more than three or four miles from the opposite side. An hour's walk will take you across it in a straight line—provided you can find a straight line. In much of the city, the streets wind, and when intersections occur, they are often at anything but right angles. When one landmark is described as being close to another, it may be only an eighth or a quarter of a mile away. But unless the visitor follows his map closely, he may walk a mile through unnecessary streets and over unnecessary hills to reach his destination around the corner.

The Tiber, which has played so important a part in the history of Rome, is the second largest river in Italy, but in the dry season it is a very small stream indeed, and gives a misleading impression of what it can do. In flood, it is very impressive and frightening. In the past, it has often overflowed its banks, creating havoc, and helping to spread malaria and the plague. When the water level is not too low, small steamers can come up to Rome, but when the rainfall is scanty there is little river traffic. More

23

than two thousand years ago the Romans used Ostia, which is at the river mouth, fourteen miles to the west and south, as their seaport. Since then, the river has deposited enormous quantities of silt, and Rome is almost four miles farther from the sea than in the early days. It is still a short drive to Ostia and to its neighboring Lido di Roma (Beach of Rome).

The Tiber is crossed by about twenty-four bridges, the exact number depending on how far up and down stream you count, whether you include railroad bridges, and so on. A smaller river, the Aniene or Anio, meets the Tiber in the northern part of the city. The waters of both the Tiber and the Aniene once contributed to the creation of marshes, where mosquitos flourished, and malaria was bred.

The hot summer afternoons and relatively cool nights have produced a pattern of daily life that is maintained in Rome for most of the year. Work goes on from about eight-thirty in the morning until about one in the afternoon. Then almost everything shuts down for three hours —shops, banks, even airline offices. During this break, most Romans eat a leisurely lunch or dinner and take a siesta. Work begins again at four in the afternoon and may go on till about eight. The final meal will then be eaten at about nine, in the cool of the evening and, in the summer, preferably outdoors.

It is a way of life that makes hot weather far more endurable than it is in New York, or Chicago, or Washington, D.C., although it is sometimes disconcerting to the visitor who cannot get a haircut or buy a pair of shoes when he wants them. Here and there one finds the pattern modified, as when sightseeing buses leave for tours at three in the afternoon. Most Romans take it so seriously, however, that they suffer through four traffic jams a day instead of the two customary in American cities—not only the usual race to work in the morning and back home in the late afternoon, but the rushes to and from a meal and siesta at home as well.

Like people who live in a large capital city anywhere, many Romans work in the offices of large industrial concerns, banks, and national organizations. Here they carry on the detailed business of the city, province, and nation. The most important newspapers, magazines, and book publishing houses are also located here, the Vatican alone publishing books in dozens of languages. Sometimes it seems that a good part of its population is engaged in making the many movies that are filmed in Rome itself or in the Cinecittà, the studios of which are on the outskirts of Rome.

Rome is not one of the great industrial centers—those are in the north of Italy—but its fashion industry ranks next to that of Paris and it has, either within the city limits or on the outskirts, a large number of small plants that manufacture products as varied as penicillin and other drugs and chemicals, textiles, some leather goods, electrical equipment, and food products. It employs many people in transportation and it is filled with small shops from end to end.

Like working people elsewhere, most Romans have to travel to their work. Many business and professional

New, moderate-priced apartment houses

people live in the Parioli district in the northern part of the city; or along the Tiber; or in several other comfortable neighborhoods. The ordinary working people are scattered, some living near the center of town in small buildings between shops and palaces, others on the right side of the Tiber, and still others in comparatively new government-supported low-rent apartment houses on the outskirts.

Family life in Rome has been traditionally close-knit and relaxed, although the growing pressures of a crowded city and such modern developments as the automobile and television are producing changes. For the younger children, there are not only the schools to keep them busy, but parks, gardens and playgrounds, the zoo, and the visiting circuses, which come from all over Europe. The teen-ager is more likely to be interested in sports, movies, and more adult entertainment. He may have his own informal group of friends, or may belong to the youth groups organized by the Church or by political parties. Except for the language he speaks, he differs surprisingly little from the American teenager. He too studies his lessons with the radio or TV on. Even the subtle differences of clothes and cut of hair are disappearing as new fashions sweep more and more rapidly across the world.

There is one difference, however, that is worth noting. The standard of living in Italy, although rising, is, for the average

Children at a puppet show in the Pincio

A typical scene in one of Rome's many parks

family, still far below that of the United States, and every possible breadwinner must earn what he can. Those young people who attend trade schools, instead of taking academic courses, go to work at an earlier age than their American counterparts.

Their parents lived through Fascism and through a great war, and they themselves were born in times when human life seemed worth little. Rome underwent the horrors of German occupation and, after its liberation by American troops, had to go through a painful process of reconstruction. Consequently, many young Romans, like other European young people, are more interested in political events than American teen-agers are.

Despite the intrusions of modern life, visitors continue to find Rome a comfortable and easy-going city. Shopping and eating are both done at a leisurely pace. The number of large department stores is growing, but most of the shopping is done in small stores that specialize in a few kinds of items. Roman stores do not have the variety of mass-produced goods to be found in large American cities —anything made of nylon or other synthetic fibers, for instance, is likely to be expensive. For some reason, phonograph records generally cost more than records in the United States. But many of the articles produced in Italy are of fine quality and are helping to make Rome a new fashion center.

Food is bought at small stands in open-air markets or at tiny grocery stores instead of at giant supermarkets. When Romans eat outside their homes, it is usually at small restaurants (although one may find an occasional

*From top to bottom: delicatessen, outdoor market,
and sidewalk café*

29

cafeteria, called Tavola Calda, or hot table). In many of these restaurants meals are excellent, and dishes are served in a variety of styles, corresponding to the methods of preparation in different provinces. Restaurants are called Trattoria or Ristorante. The first is an informal, inexpensive eating place, while the latter is generally more elegant as well as expensive.

Rome is already the movie capital of Europe, and the cultural and artistic center of Italy. As the seat of the government of Italy, it has many ministries and offices. It contains a great stadium, built for the Olympics of 1960, a great University, a number of hospitals, and many scientific laboratories.

One of the ironies of Roman life is its language. Modern Italian is of course descended from Latin, the language of ancient Rome. During the Middle Ages, however, as the Roman Empire disintegrated, and Italy split into small dukedoms, principalities, and city states, each area developed its own dialect. It was the Tuscan dialect, not the Roman, that became the basis for modern Italian.

Rome is a city of parks and gardens. The grounds of the Villa Borghese contain not only a museum and beautiful trees and walk, but a *Galoppatoio*, or riding ground for horses, as well. Romans have always enjoyed horses. (remember the chariot races in *Ben Hur*). The Emperor Caligula was so fond of one of his horses that he made the animal a consul of Rome, to the dismay of the human Senate.

In more modern times, the Via del Corso (Street of

Galoppatoio at Villa Borghese

the Course) was the scene of horse races from the Porta del Popolo (Gate of the People) to the Palazzo Venezia (Venetian Palace). Modern traffic being what it is, the races have been discontinued, but the Romans still show their love of animals in other ways. In the tradition of St. Francis of Assisi, who regarded every beast and bird as his brother, on January 17, San Antonio's Day, the priests give their blessings to the animals. The parks are alive with birds, and small lizards and squirrels romp over rocks, ruins, and trees.

Perhaps the animals are the only creatures in Rome that have no sense of history. The Villa Borghese was built in the early seventeenth century by two members of the Borghese family, one known as Pope Paul V, the

31

The lake's garden at Villa Borghese

other, his nephew, Cardinal Scipione Borghese. A century and a half ago it was the home of Princess Paolina Borghese, who was, before her marriage, Pauline Bonaparte. Pauline was a sister of Napoleon, who had made himself Emperor of France, and like most of Napoleon's family, she shared his good fortune. Napoleon invaded Italy, and in 1800 proclaimed himself its King. He made his stepson Viceroy of Italy, and his brother, Joseph, King of Naples. Under the circumstances, the least Pauline could expect to be was a princess. She displeased her imperial brother, however, and scandalized the noble Borghese family into which she had married, when she posed for a nude statue. This is now in the museum, where it attracts unscandalized visitors.

It is not only the famous places that forcibly remind one of the past. An old apartment house may turn out to be a former palace. So may the bank where the visitor changes his travelers' checks, or the library from which the Roman borrows his books. Every old street and old house has seen and been seen by illustrious men and women. From the north, over the Ponte Milvio (Milvian Bridge), down the Via Flaminia (see next page), and through the Porta del Popolo into Rome have come the bearers of great and historic names—Martin Luther, Raphael (Raffaello), the German poet Goethe, the French essayist Montaigne, English poets such as Byron, Shelley, and Keats; popes, kings, and princes without number. Dead indeed is the spirit of the visitor who treads the same ground and is not thrilled by the recollection of such a past.

Flaminian Way—ancient, at left; modern, at right

THREE HILLS

The millions of people who worshipped Apollo, Diana, and Venus have been dead for centuries and, all over Rome, Christian churches have triumphed over pagan temples. But on the Capitoline (Capitolino), the smallest of the seven hills, one can still summon the spirit of the pagan past. For here dwelt Jupiter, king of the gods, and here the Romans erected a temple in his name. Victorious generals ascended the hill after their triumphs, dressed to resemble Jupiter himself, with the laurel crowns of victors on their heads, and the purple togas of kings and gods on their bodies.

According to the legends, Romulus, wishing to provide more soldiers for his new city, proclaimed a Sanctuary, or place of refuge, on the Capitoline. To it he called together outlaws, exiles, and fugitives from all over Italy. In a new environment, these outcasts of Italian society became new men, and their descendants were later to be celebrated for their virtues.

People dwelt on the slopes of the Capitoline, but no village appears to have been built on top of the hill, which had two summits. The Capitoline served other purposes. The summit on the north side became the Arx, or Citadel, where people gathered for refuge in time of war. Alongside the Citadel was the temple of Juno Moneta, Juno the Warner. On one celebrated occasion, during a stealthy night attack by the Gauls, the cackling of Juno's geese alerted the garrison and saved the Citadel. Although geese have been honored in Rome since that night, their honors do not prevent them from being eaten. Of Arx and the temple, nothing now remains.

The Tarpeian Rock (Rupe Tarpeia) which faces west, was named in grim memory of Tarpeia, priestess of Vesta, who betrayed the Citadel to the Sabines. Tarpeia demanded as her reward what the Sabines wore on their left arms—their golden bracelets. The Sabines deliberately misinterpreted her words to mean their shields, also carried in their left arms, and tossed these upon her, crushing her to death. According to a more prosaic version of the legend, it was Spurius Tarpeius, her father, who was the traitor, and he was supposedly thrown from the rock. Tarpeia was buried at the foot of the hill below the rock. Later the Romans used the Tarpeian Rock as a place of execution, hurling to their deaths those convicted of crimes against the state.

Many of the myths and legends of early Rome have the Capitoline and its two neighboring hills, the Palatine (Palatino) and the Aventine (Aventino), as their background. Romulus and Remus were supposed to have been suckled by the she-wolf in a marshy spot near the Aventine. The Roman historian Livy says that Romulus founded the city on the Palatine. On this hill, in fact, still stand the walls of a so-called House of Romulus.

The first inhabitants of the area, however, predated even the kings of legend. Archaeologists have found, on several of the hills, including the Palatine, remains of villages built as far back as the ninth and tenth centuries B.C. The tribes who inhabited these villages were conquered by the Etruscans, a neighboring people, who united the small settlements into a single town and surrounded it with a wall which was later attributed to Romulus. About 500 B.C., the Romans overthrew Etruscan rule, killed the last Etruscan king, and established a republic.

By this time the character of the Capitoline had become established. Revered as the home of Jupiter, it was also hated as the stronghold from which the overbearing Etruscans ruled the city. Its name was derived from *caput*, the Latin word for head, and has given us our "Capitol," the chief government building in a state or in a country. The symbolic significance of the Capitoline was great. From the early days of the Republic, the Romans kept a sharp eye on those members of their new ruling class, called patricians, who might aspire to become kings or absolute dictators. Any man who wanted to build a home on the Capitoline was immediately suspect.

Despite their early watchfulness, the Romans eventually lost their freedom to rulers who became not merely kings but emperors. As time went on, the character of the Capitoline changed. The temple of Jupiter Capitolinus fell into ruins, as did the Citadel. In the early years of Christianity, a church was built on the north summit,

Church of Santa Maria d'Aracoeli

where the temple of Juno had once stood. Largely rebuilt in the fourteenth century, this is famous as the church of Santa Maria d'Aracoeli (St. Mary of the Altar of Heaven). It can be reached by a long, steep flight of steps from the bottom of the hill, or by a shorter flight from the level of the Capitol Square.

Most of the modern Capitoline we owe to Michelangelo. Michelangelo Buonarroti (1474–1564) was the most famous artist of his day. Painter, sculptor, and architect, he was the pride of Rome, not merely because he lived there but because he added so much to the beauty of the city. We shall meet much of his work elsewhere, notably in the Vatican. He designed and began the construction of the Piazza del Campidoglio, on the south summit.

The ground of the Square is covered with tile arranged in beautiful mosaic patterns. (See picture, page 41.) On the Square is the Capitoline Museum (Museo), which contains such well-known statues as the Dying Gaul, the Wounded Amazon, and the Capitoline Venus. Another museum on the Capitoline, the Palazzo dei Conservatori (the Palace of the Councillors), contains equally famous sculpture, Boy Extracting a Thorn, and the She-Wolf among others.

On the Capitoline too is the Palazzo Senatorio, or Senatorial Palace, the City Hall of Rome, built on top of the ancient Tabulario, or record hall, where official documents were kept. Here is the office of the *Sindaco*, or Mayor, and of important departments of the city administration. Public announcements and notices of forth-

Tabulario or, as it is usually called, Tabularium

coming marriages are posted on the walls. In this area, city servants mingle with crowds of visitors and, among the great buildings and works of art, one finds the bustle and life of modern Rome.

Outdoors, in the Square of the Capitol, are several famous statues. Of greatest renown is a statue of the Emperor Marcus Aurelius on horseback. Placed here in 1538, this work was preserved for centuries under the illusion that it was a statue of Constantine, the first Christian emperor, and it has inspired similar statues by the sculptors of the Renaissance. At the head of a staircase built by Michelangelo, the Dioscuri, or twin gods, Castor and Pollux, stand alongside their horses. Castor and Pollux were especially revered because, during a battle in 496 B.C., they were seen helping the Romans on to victory. The two pieces of sculpture were found in the Roman

Capitol Square, showing mosaic tile and Marcus Aurelius statue

Michelangelo staircase with Castor and Pollux statues

Ghetto, the Jewish quarter, and brought to the Campidoglio in 1583. There is a statue of a she-wolf suckling the infants in the Campidoglio, and a few feet below the statues of Castor and Pollux, off to one side, is the live she-wolf mentioned earlier.

From the Capitoline one can look down on much of the city. At the foot of the eastern slope is what remains of the Roman Forum—the ruins of ancient arches and columns and of magnificent buildings, with a narrow lane called the Via Sacra, or Sacred Way, winding among them. Along this much-revered road marched triumphal processions with their booty and their captives, the latter often destined for sacrifice in honor of the gods.

The Roman Forum was a place where comedy and tragedy were played daily in real life, where everything in Rome that was amusing, exciting, and horrifying either happened or was talked about. It was the center of Roman life and liveliness.

Via Sacra

Live she-wolf in her cage

For its existence we must thank the Etruscans. *Forum* means *out of doors*, and this particular out-of-doors spot was a marsh between the Palatine and Capitoline hills, which the Etruscans drained. Because of its convenient location, it soon became a marketplace, where peasants and artisans met to barter their goods, and bankers and merchants set up shop. People began to come here not only to buy and sell, but to meet friends, to listen to speeches and debates, and to take part in the religious and political life of the city. Temples were built, along with a Curia, or Senate building. Emperors constructed memorials and, as the area became insufficient for the administration of a large city, added other forums.

During the decline of the Roman Empire, these buildings were destroyed and plundered for their marble and other building stone. Later on, the Forum became a Campo Vaccino, or Cow Pasture. Today it is the site of some of the most rewarding ruins in Rome, where archaeologists dig into the history of the past.

Eight columns mark what is left of the Temple of Saturn, standing at the foot of the Capitoline. Saturn was the god who supposedly ruled the province of Latium (Lazio), where Rome is situated. In December of each year the Romans celebrated his rites, some with prayer and sacrifice, others in wild orgies. During this period, known as the Saturnalia, religious processions made their way to the Temple of Saturn.

Three columns are left of the Temple of Castor and Pollux, while nearby, in the center of the Forum, are a few ruins of the House of the Vestal Virgins (Casa delle

Vestali). Vesta, the goddess of the hearth and hearth-fire, was in some respects the most honored of all Roman deities, and worship of her was part of the official religion.

A short distance away, there is a single, ancient column, on top of which a gilded statue was later added. This prominent feature of the Forum is a testimonial to the imaginary virtues of the tyrant Phocas (Foca), then reigning over the Roman Empire from the city of Byzantium, later to be known as Constantinople. An admirer, Smaragdus, a Byzantine, was responsible for the statue and its inscription praising the Emperor for bringing peace and liberty to Italy. What Phocas had actually brought were death and destruction, but Smaragdus, who owed his own position as ruler of the province to the Emperor, mentioned only his virtues.

A considerable part of the Forum was devoted to commemorating victory in war and its bloody aftermath. Three arches, dedicated to Settimio Severo (Septimius Severus), Constantine, and Tito (Titus), are among those that can be seen from the Capitoline (see next page). That of Septimius Severus honors the Emperor and his sons for their victories in Asia. Constantine is honored for his defeat of the rival Roman Emperor, Maxentius (Massenzio), and his seizure of uncontested power. The arch of Titus commemorates the taking of Jerusalem and the slaughter of its inhabitants.

Near the Arch of Septimius Severus are the remains of a state prison, known in early times as the Tullianum, and later as the Mamertine Prison. Among the famous

Arch of Constantine

Detail of Arch of Titus

St. Paul's Outside the Walls

prisoners were Jugurtha, King of Numidia, and Vercingetorix, chief of the Gauls, who was defeated by Julius Caesar. Jugurtha died in the prison, while Vercingetorix was led along the Via Sacra in Caesar's triumph and executed after six years of captivity. Here, too, Saints Peter and Paul were said to have been imprisoned. Both were executed later, St. Paul not far from the church outside the walls which bears his name.

Among the more peaceful sights in the Forum are the remains of the Golden Milestone (Miliarium Aureum), a column set up by the Emperor Augustus as the point from which all Roman roads were to be measured. The Forum also contains the Umbilicus Urbis, the Navel of the City, a stone which supposedly marks the center of Rome. Near the Umbilicus is the Lapis Niger, or Black Stone, said in ancient times to cover the grave of Romulus. Excavators have found under it remains that go back to about 600 B.C.

Very little on the surface of the Forum, or elsewhere

47

in Rome, for that matter, dates so far back, chiefly because of the invasion by the Gauls in 390 B.C.

The Romans had not only invasion to contend with, but their own internal struggles. For five centuries after the expulsion of the Etruscan kings, while spreading their rule first through Italy and then over the entire area of the Mediterranean, the Romans fought among themselves. Republican in form, Rome was ruled by the patrician upper class, against whom the plebians, or lower class, fought continually for greater freedom.

In this battle the upper class usually had the upper hand, although their position slowly became more and more insecure. Power fell gradually into the hands of their generals, themselves patricians. The generals became dictators, ruling by military force alone, with little pretense of legality. The process reached its climax with Julius Caesar, who was the first to attain absolute power. Caesar was assassinated by other patricians, but it was already too late to save the republic, and Caesar's nephew, Octavius, after defeating his chief rival, Marc Antony, assumed the title of Emperor and the name Augustus.

It was to the Forum that the body of Caesar was brought to lie in state while Marc Antony made his famous funeral oration, inciting the people against the assassins. But before he died, Caesar had started to build another Forum, which Augustus completed and named for him. Caesar also began the large Basilica Giulia, likewise completed by Augustus. (A basilica was a large oblong building used for trials and meetings. Later the name was applied to Christian churches of the same shape.)

Basilica of St. Maxentius

Still standing in the Forum is the Basilica of Maxentius, named for the emperor who began its construction. Sometimes called the Basilica of Constantine, after the emperor who conquered Maxentius and finished the building, it is used today as a great open-air concert hall.

As the buildings of the Forum increased in number, they spread not only to the north, where they became the Imperial Forums, but also up the slope of the Palatine. This hill, which had been inhabited from the early days of the city, even before the date ascribed to Romulus, soon had on it the elaborate homes, known as *palaces*, of the wealthier and more aristocratic families.

Later on, the emperors built there, beginning with Augustus, who took over a wealthy man's home and added new buildings of his own. Much of his palace,

Palatine Hill

called the House of Augustus, or more frequently the
House of Livia (his wife) still stands. Some of the later
emperors lived in the same palace, and others—Tiberio,
Caligula, and Domiziano (Domitian)—built palaces of
their own. Caligula, who was insane, was murdered here,
and so was Domitian, hated for his cruelty. The Emperor
Heliogabalus (Eliogabalo), a perverted young man with
a perverse sense of humor, would invite his friends to a
magnificent banquet and then add spice to the meal by
turning lions and leopards loose among them.

The Capitol and the Forum should be seen at least
twice, for they look quite different in moonlight and in
bright sun. The ruins of the Forum assume a still different
appearance when they are lit up artificially, as they are
for several hours each evening.

In the Middle Ages, the Frangipani, a family of well-

born bandits, built a fortress on the Palatine, ascending
from the Arch of Titus far up the hill. From this haven
they raided the surrounding countryside, robbing and
killing. Among their exploits was the capture and imprisonment of a Pope, whom they held for ransom. Centuries later, the once dreaded name of Frangipani was
still remembered—but chiefly as the designation of a pow-
erful floral perfume.

Today the medieval fortress is completely gone, and
the ancient palaces are in ruins, some of them in fairly
good condition as ruins go. The Casino Farnese was built
on the Palatine years later, and the garden and fountain
still survive. One of the emperors had orchards here, and
much of the Palatine has become a botanical garden,
where pines, cypresses, orange trees, and pomegranate
trees flourish, along with many rare plants.

Separated from the Capitoline and the Palatine by a narrow valley called the Velabro, or Golden Veil, is the Aventine, a much larger hill that stretches along the Tiber. Between the Palatine and the Aventine once stood the Circo Massimo (Circus Maximus, meaning Greatest Circle). This was an amphitheatre where once the Emperors kept the Roman citizens amused. Here two hundred thousand spectators could assemble to watch chariot races. Nothing of the Circo Massimo remains.

The Aventine is a hill of peace, a quiet retreat in a busy city. Children play in the Parco Savello, named for the family of that name, under the shade of orange and pine trees, while their elders gaze out across the Tiber at one of the most beautiful views of a city famed for its views. The Basilica of Santa Sabina stands near the park, where a temple of a pagan goddess once stood.

Within a few steps of the church is the Garden of the Cavalieri di Malta (Knights of Malta). This is closed to the general public; nevertheless scores of people visit it each day. If you put your eye to the keyhole of the garden gate, you can see, framed by two rows of trees, the dome of St. Peter's Basilica, some three-quarters of a mile away. The sight is as unexpected as it is fascinating, and Romans bring their children to enjoy it.

Some of the more elegant Roman houses are found here. Twenty-five centuries ago, however, it was the scene of Bacchic orgies held by a secret society, and of human sacrifice. On one occasion it almost witnessed the end of Rome when, after a quarrel with the patricians, the plebians withdrew to this spot and threatened to secede from

Entrance to the garden of the Knights of Malta
(Note the typical wine cart in the piazza)

Dome of St. Peter's Basilica seen through the keyhole

San Giorgio in Velabro (from an old print)

the city. Only after an apology from their rulers did the plebians return.

On the Aventine, near the Porta San Paolo (St. Paul's Gate), is the Piramide Caio Cestio (Pyramid of Caius Cestius), with the city wall built right up to it. A short distance beyond is the Cimitero Protestante (Protestant Cemetery), where Keats and Shelley are buried.

The area surrounded by the three hills is now busy with traffic. Two of the famous churches of Rome are here: San Giorgio in Velabro (St. George in the Velabrum) and Santa Maria in Cosmedin (St. Mary Adorned). San Giorgio in Velabro is the same St. George the English consider their protector.

The two churches are on opposite sides of a famous square named Piazza Bocca della Verità (Mouth of Truth). This receives its name from the curious large round marble face in the portico of Santa Maria in Cosmedin. During

54

Santa Maria in Cosmedin

late Roman times, and in the Middle Ages, people swore oaths with one hand in the Bocca della Verità. The Mouth was supposed to bite the hand of a liar. To the community around it, the church was better known as the church of the Bocca than by its own name.

These three hills symbolize the survival of the past, as it mingles with the present, making of Rome many cities in one.

La Bocca della Verità

III.

A FIELD AND SOME FOUNTAINS

Julius Caesar had a bold idea for the expansion of Rome. In his day, the city proper did not include the area within the loop of the Tiber between the Porta del Popolo and the Capitoline Hill. The land, which is the Campus Martius, mentioned earlier, had belonged to the Etruscan kings and after them to the Republic and, although some temples were built there, the construction of private homes was forbidden. It was used as a drill ground for the army, and later as a polling place. Caesar planned to build homes there and to turn the river aside to create a new Martian Field where Vatican City now is.

Caesar's plan was vetoed by the daggers of his assassins, and the river remained in its old bed. Nevertheless, the pressure of the city's growth forced the Romans to build in the Martian Field and the surrounding area. Although, like every other part of Rome, it has its relics of the past, today it is one of the busiest and liveliest sections of the city.

The Porta del Popolo is flanked by the Church of Santa Maria del Popolo, built on the reputed burial spot of the Emperor Nero, who persecuted the early Christians, and was supposed to have fiddled while Rome burned. The building of the church was intended to exorcise the spirit of Nero, which was said to hover in a tree alongside the gates. The church was first constructed in 1099 and has since been rebuilt several times. It is as much museum as religious edifice, and works by such great artists as Raphael, Michelangelo da Caravaggio, and Gian Lorenzo Bernini adorn it. It has been attended by the noted and notorious of all centuries. It was to this church that Lucrezia Borgia, who probably did not deserve her ill repute as a poisoner, came to give thanks for her betrothal to her third husband. People have thought the worst of Lucrezia because she was a daughter of Pope Alexander VI and sister of Cesare Borgia, a killer in his own right.

If the spirit of the wicked Nero was driven from his grave, it apparently did not go far, for the adjoining square, the Piazza del Popolo, was for centuries a place of execution that would have made any Roman Emperor feel at home. The death sentence was applied not only to criminals and unfortunate victims of persecution, but often, accidentally, to the spectators as well, when the stands built for such festive occasions collapsed, killing and injuring many.

Located directly below another of Rome's hills, the Pincio (Pincian Hill), the Piazza del Popolo is just inside the protective wall built around the city in the third century A.D. by the Emperor Aurelian. Its obelisk was brought to Rome even earlier, by the Emperor Augustus. Used in recent years for political rallies, the Piazza del

Piazza del Popolo

Popolo is now also popular as a meeting place for artists, who congregate in rival groups in the outdoor cafés or restaurants, either in the Piazza itself or in the streets around it. Many artists have their studios in Via Margutta, to the east of the Piazza.

As we leave the Piazza to enter the Via del Corso, we pass between the twin churches of Santa Maria dei Miracoli and Santa Maria di Montesanto (St. Mary of the Miracles and St. Mary of the Holy Hill). A number of architects were involved in their planning and building, and their ideas did not always harmonize, but the result is, nonetheless, a beautiful one.

The Corso is an extension of the old Flaminian Way, and was for centuries the chief street of Rome. Goethe, the most famous of German poets, lived on it, as did Shelley. Once known as Via Lata, or Broad Street, and later as Via Umberto I, it is still one of the most notable streets in the city. For a Broad Street it is remarkably narrow, and the horses who raced along it must have suffered many collisions. It is now lined with shops that sell medium-priced articles, and with office buildings. It is about a mile long, running into the Piazza Venezia.

In the old Palazzo Venezia, overlooking this square, Benito Mussolini made his headquarters. From the balcony he addressed the "oceans of volunteers" who had been forced to fill the square to listen to him as he painted word pictures of a new Rome that would once more possess the entire Mediterranean area for its empire. The pictures were false; Mussolini himself betrayed Italy to the Germans. Perhaps he was haunted by memories of

Palazzo Venezia, showing
"Mussolini's balcony"

another empire, for the Piazza Venezia owed its existence to Charles VIII of France, who in his time possessed Rome instead of being possessed by it. Charles VIII terrorized the city and tore down the houses in this district to make a parade ground for his artillery.

If we leave the Piazza del Popolo to the right of the Corso, we pass along the Via di Ripetta through a section of relatively modern buildings to reach Piazza Augusto Imperatore (Emperor Augustus Square), with its tomb of Augustus. Around 13 B.C., after accomplishing his aims by war and establishing Roman rule in Gaul and Spain, Augustus built an Altar of Peace (Ara Pacis), which can still be seen near his tomb.

About a half mile south of Piazza Augusto, in the old Martian Field, is the very large and beautiful Piazza Navona on the site of a stadium built for athletic contests—chiefly chariot races—by the Emperor Domitian. This is

Piazza Navona, with Fontana dei Fiumi and outdoor market

the center of an area crowded with old buildings, and at times so many small children and parents fill the piazza that the kindergartens and grammar schools appear to be having a convention. Sant'Agnese in Agone Church stands in this piazza, as do the Palazzo Pamphili and the Brazilian Embassy. The cafés around Piazza Navona are favored by musicians as well as by other Romans and visitors.

Piazza Navona is celebrated for its three fountains, of which the largest is the Fontana dei Fiumi (Fountain of the Rivers). This highly ornamented masterpiece, the work of Gian Lorenzo Bernini, portrays symbolically the Danube, Nile, Ganges, and La Plata rivers. The fountain is topped by an obelisk, which is hardly needed to bring it to the visitor's attention (see page 11). Nearby is the Fontana del Moro (Fountain of the Moor) also by Bernini.

Bernini, born in Naples in 1598, lived to the age of eighty-one, and produced a tremendous amount of sculpture and architecture. He accomplished so much because he started young, producing his first well-known piece of sculpture at the age of sixteen. By the time he was about twenty-three he was successful enough to hire others to help him carve his stone and cast his bronze. The executors of his ideas were often master sculptors in their own right.

But if, in this respect, Bernini did less than he is usually credited with, in other respects he did more. He wrote a number of comedies, and created the stage designs for them. And on at least one occasion he built a theatre, composed music to his own comedy, painted the scenery and adorned the stage with his own statues, invented intricate backstage machinery to produce special effects, and even sang a part or two in his own opera.

One of the colorful streets in this area that still seems to retain its medieval character is Via dei Coronari (Street of the Garlandmakers) who once lived and worked here. It is still a working-class street, as are many of the streets in this neighborhood. Washing hangs from lines, sometimes next door to old palaces, and antique hunters seek bargains in the small shops.

The Piazza Navona was formerly known as the Circlo Agonale (Circle for Combat). The foundations of the ancient stadium can still be seen in the cellars of some of the houses there, and the entire piazza is an outstanding example of Baroque architecture.

Between the Piazza Navona and the Corso is the Pantheon, a temple to "all the gods," first built in 27 B.C.

Pantheon

Elephant and obelisk in Piazza della Minerva

The Romans left it without a closed roof to permit the gods to enter, but the old deities have been shut out by its conversion into a church, Sancta Maria ad Martyres, a name conferred upon it when thousands of martyrs were exhumed from the Catacombs and reburied here. A fountain topped by an obelisk stands in front of it. The Pantheon is also famous as the tomb of Raphael. After the restoration of a kingdom of Italy in the late nineteenth century, it became the burial place of the Italian royal family, two kings and a queen keeping Raphael company within the walls.

A short distance away is the Piazza della Minerva, and alongside this the church of Santa Maria Sopra Minerva. The name, St. Mary Above Minerva, is a triple play on words, indicating the triumph of St. Mary over the heathen goddess of wisdom, the construction of a church on the site of an ancient temple to Minerva, and the fact that the

church overlooks Minerva Square. The temple was built
by Pompey, whose defeat by Julius Caesar preceded the
defeat of his goddess by St. Mary. In the square stands an
odd creation of Bernini's, an elephant carrying an obelisk.
This is symbolic and is supposed to prove that only the
strength of an elephant can support the weight of soaring
wisdom. The visitor may draw his own conclusions.

Closer to the river, in the region of the Martian Field,
are a number of buildings interesting both on their own
account and for their historical associations. The pleasant
church of Sant'Andrea della Valle, on Corso Vittorio
Emanuele, is not far from the Palazzo Farnese, a Renaissance masterpiece completed by Michelangelo, and now
used as the French Embassy. The church is the scene of
the first act of the opera *Tosca*, the Palazzo the scene of
the second act. Forming the third angle of a small triangle
with these two buildings is the Cancelleria (Chancellory).

Courtyard of the Cancelleria

The property of the Vatican, this is another fine example of a Renaissance palace—so fine, in fact, that it was taken over by Napoleon when he captured Rome more than a century and a half ago. Within the triangle is the Piazza Campo dei Fiori (Field of Flowers Square) which contains a fruit market.

Near these buildings is the Largo di Torre Argentina. Here are the remains of temples of republican Rome and the homes of hundreds of cats. The Teatro Argentina, where Rossini's opera *The Barber of Seville* was first produced in 1816, is still in use in this area. Not far away, on Piazza Cavour, named for the Italian Premier who was the first to succeed in the unification of Italy, is the Minis-

tero Grazia e Giustizia (Ministry of Pardon and Justice), a government building. Even closer to the Largo Argentina is Piazza Mattei, a small square that contains the famous Fontana delle Tartarughe (Fountain of the Tortoises).

Right off the Corso itself is the Piazza Colonna (Column Square). The column was raised in 174 A.D. to commemorate the victories of the Emperor Marcus Aurelius. Centuries later, in 1589, Pope Sixtus V replaced the statue of the pagan emperor with a statue of St. Paul, which now looks down upon the Romans and their visitors. (See next page.)

At the southern tip of the old Martian Field, in the morning shadow of the Campidoglio, near the former Ghetto of Rome, is the Theatre of Marcellus (Teatro

Piazza Cavour and Ministry of Justice

*Column in
Column Square
(Piazza Colonna)*

Marcello (see page 69), one of the structures begun by Julius Caesar, left uncompleted at his death, and completed by Augustus. The latter named it for his adopted son, who died young and was much lamented. Its top floor has been rebuilt, so that it now serves as an apartment house. In medieval times it was one of the buildings used as fortresses by families such as the Frangipanis. Eagles and wolves are kept in cages at the foot of the rocks nearby to symbolize the eagles of Rome, on the standards carried by the legions, and, of course, the wolf that suckled Romulus and Remus.

If we start again at the Porta del Popolo and take the road to the left, we find ourselves on the Via del Babuino (Baboon Street), lined with shops and offices. The Italian broadcasting system has its headquarters here. In the area between the Corso and Via

Theatre of Marcellus

del Babuino is Via Vittoria (Victory Street), where the Academy of St. Cecilia is dedicated to the patron saint of music. Homage is paid St. Cecilia in frequent concerts. Nearby is Via Condotti (Conduit Street), along which water is piped to some of the fountains.

Via Condotti now boasts some of the most elegant shops in Rome. It is one of the streets that lead into Piazza di Spagna, the Spanish Square, which received its name from the Spanish Embassy to the Vatican, located near the foot of the impressive and much photographed Scala di Spagna (the Spanish Steps). These were built in 1726 and lead to the church of Santissima Trinità dei Monti

(Holy Trinity of the Mountains). The fountain in the center of the Piazza di Spagna is in the form of a boat, and was built by Pietro Bernini, father of the more famous Gian Lorenzo Bernini. Among the houses on each side of the Spanish Steps were the homes of Keats, Shelley, and Byron. A house in the piazza at the foot of the steps has been turned into a memorial for Keats and Shelley.

Turning toward the Corso again, we reach the Piazza San Silvestro, a busy square that serves as a bus terminal in the center of the city. This square has many small shops, and the main post office of Rome is located here in an old convent. A few blocks from the Piazza Colonna and the Piazza San Silvestro is the Fontana di Trevi, which is two hundred years old. The name is a contraction of *Tre Vie* (Three Ways), referring to the fountain's three main outlets. The water flows over and around statues of Neptune, Health, and Fertility, unexpected pagan deities to encounter in a fountain built under the rule of the Popes. It is an attraction not only for tourists but for the Romans themselves. Children cool their feet in it, masters bring their dogs to drink from it, and young and old use it as a meeting place. (See page 14.)

Continuing on the Corso we come to the often-pictured monument to Vittorio Emanuele II. Italy is now, of course, a republic, but Italians still honor the memory of Victor Emmanuel II because he was the symbol and the first king of the united modern country. The first Victor Emmanuel was king of Sardinia, and so was the second at the beginning of his career.

In the early part of the nineteenth century, Italy was

The Spanish Steps and Santissima Trinità dei Monti

divided into a number of small kingdoms, such as those of Sicily, Sardinia, and Naples, under the domination of Austria and France. Rome itself, along with several other provinces, was ruled by the Pope. A number of movements for the liberation and unity of Italy failed before Victor Emmanuel II was proclaimed King of Italy in 1861. Much fighting and negotiating followed, before, in 1866, the Austrians yielded Venezia, the province of which Venice is the chief city, and before 1870, when the French withdrew from Rome, which was then taken from the Pope and became the capital of Italy.

If Victor Emmanuel was the symbol of a united Italy, Giuseppe Garibaldi was its hero. Born in Nice, France, in 1807, Garibaldi took part in an unsuccessful rebellion in Genoa in 1834, and was condemned to death. He fled, to become a soldier in South America, fighting on the side of the weak new republic of Uruguay against Argentina. In 1848, a year of revolution throughout Europe, he returned to Italy to fight for freedom again. Again he failed, and again he went abroad, first to Africa and then to the United States. But as the years passed, the Italian will to achieve unity was growing. When once more Garibaldi returned, he captured Sicily, and marched into Naples. Later on, he made two attempts to capture Rome, and would have succeeded if the French had not come to the aid of the Pope. Rome was finally taken in 1870, and Italy at last had its capital. Garibaldi now joined forces with his former enemies, the French, against the Prussians in the Franco-Prussian war. Garibaldi's patriotism put him on the side of freedom everywhere. He had the distinction of being elected to both the French National Assembly and the Italian Parliament.

In later years, the name of Victor Emmanuel lost much of its lustre because of the behavior of Victor Emmanuel III. This Victor Emmanuel was the third king of Italy, and earned the contempt of many Italians when he allowed, or possibly helped, the Fascists under Mussolini to seize power and turn Italy into a dictatorship. After World War II, with Mussolini hanged and the Fascists driven from power, the Italians voted for a republic. The great majority of the people despise the Fascists and would fight their return to power, as indeed many partisans fought against them during the war, but there is a small neo-Fascist party of diehards who look back to the past and long for a return of their special privileges.

At any rate, the Vittoriano, or the "wedding cake," as many Italians call the Victor Emmanuel Monument, is a dazzling white edifice that stands before the Campidoglio (as one looks down the Corso) with the Piazza

Monument to Victor Emmanuel II—"the wedding cake"

Venezia in front of it. It was started in 1885 and completed in 1911. The mountain of labor spent in building it brought forth, in the opinion of some Romans, not a mouse but a monstrosity. Whatever may be thought about its beauty, there is no doubt that it catches the eye, and even inhabitants who consider it a crime against art have acquired a peculiar pride in it, just as some Chicagoans refer with a peculiar pride to the criminal history of *their* city. If you must go in for bad art or for crime, they suggest, there is a certain distinction in doing it in a big way. In the monument is the tomb of Italy's Unknown Soldier.

The entire area of the former Martian Field is full, not only of the heritage of the past, but of homes, shops, and offices. These occupy old tenements, old palaces, and a number of more modern buildings. The streets are narrow, twisting, and crowded. People live here, work here, buy slices of melon from street vendors here, and rest here in the squares and beside the fountains. If the area is a pedestrian's nightmare, it is not much better for the automobile driver, who must pick his way through and around the narrow passages, guessing which will turn out to be the right one-way streets, or for the bus driver, who somehow manages to maneuver his crowded bus through streets and around corners obviously designed for the passage of horses, carriages, and ox-carts.

Sometimes the Romans think wistfully of rebuilding —but the past is too precious, and it would be impossible to straighten the streets and build a modern city without tearing down honored monuments and destroying beloved fountains and squares. No one suggests adopting the method Nero is supposed to have used in 64 A.D. Historians have argued as to whether Nero actually set fire to Rome or merely enjoyed the flames once they had been started by some accident. There had been talk of rebuilding according to some logical plan, but always too many people were interested in maintaining the *status quo*. In ancient Rome, as in modern New York and Chicago, many attempts at large-scale building were sure to be delayed, if not blocked entirely, by lawsuits.

The fire, how ever it began, settled all that. It burned for many days, and it is said that even the marble of the temples disintegrated in the intense heat. Once it had done its destructive work, rebuilding was a grim necessity.

Nero did not fiddle while Rome burned, as there were no violins in those days, and it is questionable whether he even played the lyre. He was probably too busy. He knew that people would be left without shelter, that food supplies would have been burned, and that unless he did something fast he would have a homeless, angry mob of Romans on his hands. For a wicked emperor he was sufficiently clever to be humane in his own interest. He acted immediately, setting up tents to shelter the people, and beginning at once to distribute food.

Some historians claim that all this was planned, that he had collected grain ships in Mediterranean harbors in preparation for the fire, along with the tents, and that he had even had architects draw up plans for a new Rome. It seems unlikely. But then, so do many of the things we see and hear about Rome, even when they are true.

IV.

THE OTHER FOUR HILLS

Farther in from the Tiber lie the remaining four of
the original seven hills of Rome, or what is left of them
after a great deal of excavation. To distinguish where
one ends and another begins is at times difficult. A few
streets do serve as boundary lines. Via di San Gregorio
separates the Celio (Coelian) from the Palatine, and Via
Nazionale comes between the Quirinale and the Viminale.
But, in general, as you walk along you find yourself going
up or down without always being sure whether you have
passed from one hill to another or have merely crossed
a hump on a single hill. The names do not help either.
Knowing that it was named for an Etruscan, Coelius
Vibenna, does not make it easier to identify the Coelian.
Neither does the fact that the names of the Quirinale
and Esquilino are derived from words which mean Oak
Grove. The oak trees that once were the basis for the
names, and the osiers that once gave the name Osier Hill
to the Viminale have been largely replaced by buildings.

To add to your confusion, you may be told that the
Janiculum is one of the seven hills. This is on the other

side of the river, and was not one of the original seven. It was included when Rome was an Empire, and the Capitoline was then omitted. It was also during the Empire that much of the Esquilino was dug up and the dirt carried away to make room for great buildings. You will also come upon other hills, such as Colle Oppio (Oppian Hill), which nestles among the seven hills, but is never considered one of them.

We shall therefore consider the region as a whole, as the Romans themselves did, once they began to build on a large scale. Nero, when he built a great palace with parks and gardens, had it extend from the Palatine to the area cleared by removal of part of the Esquilino, and up the slopes of the Esquilino. This vast project, known as the Golden House (Domus Aurea), was more than a mile in length, and included fields, vineyards, an artificial lake, and a zoo. It was so costly and so useless—to anyone but Nero—that it was later cited as evidence of Nero's insanity, or at least of megalomania, for the Emperor did not neglect to have a giant bronze statue of himself put up. He regarded himself as a god, of course, but then the Romans elevated all their emperors to the level of a god; Julius Caesar himself claimed descent from the goddess Venus. After a time, merely being a god did not rank very high as a status symbol. It depended on what kind of god you were.

It is possible that Nero's Golden House was built as a vast temple to his fellow Sun-god, for the worship of foreign deities had become fashionable in the Rome of his day, but this is far from certain.

*The ruins of the Baths of Trajan (above), and
Nero's Golden House (below)*

Of the Golden House, only scattered ruins are left, and these are mingled with the ruins of the Baths of Trajan (Traiano), which had been built in the same area. The lake was filled in and, on its site, shortly after Nero's death, the Colosseum was built by the labor of twelve thousand Jewish slaves. Nero contributed the popular name, derived from his "colossal" statue, and the marble, which was taken from his Golden House.

The Colosseum, whose formal name was the Flavian Amphitheatre, was a great ellipse. The arena in its center took up less than a fifth of the entire area of the building. The building had four stories, and the side facing the Oppian Park still rises to that height. The tiers had seats for possibly seventy-five thousand spectators, and beneath the floor were dressing rooms, as well as cages for wild beasts. The arena could be flooded for the staging of naval battles.

Begun by Vespasian and finished by Titus in 80 A.D., the Colosseum was used for gladiatorial games even before it was completed. At the official opening perform-

The Colosseum

ance there were displays of naval maneuvers, and thousands of animals were slain. Following a do-it-yourself fad among emperors, the Emperor Commodus used to go down into the arena to kill gladiators and wild beasts with his own hands. Or perhaps this was not a fad, but useful practice in the art of self-protection, for by this time treachery was the rule in Imperial circles, and most of the emperors could not trust their own bodyguards.

Through the years, the Colosseum is said to have become the chief arena in which Christians were tortured for the amusement of the crowd. But the Christian martyrs usually did not put up much of a struggle, and more ferocious victims were still preferred. To celebrate the thousandth anniversary of the founding of Rome, there was a special slaughter. A thousand pairs of gladiators fought to the death, and elephants, tigers, lions, and leopards, which were more expensive than gladiators, were killed off in smaller numbers.

The Colosseum, as we now see it, is a shell of its former self. It was the victim of two earthquakes that took place as long ago as the thirteenth century; its marble, or rather the marble from the Golden House, has been stripped away to be used in many of the later buildings of Rome; some of it has even been burned for lime. Even in its ruined state, it was a formidable fortress in medieval days—once used as a stronghold by the Frangipani family. Temporarily deserted by human predators, it became for a time a lair for wolves, whose depredations caused Pope Julius II to put a price upon their heads.

A short distance up a steep hill from the Colosseum

is the church of San Pietro in Vincoli (St. Peter in Chains), highly venerated for its religious relics and famous for its statue of Moses by Michelangelo. This statue has been so greatly admired that no critic can win attention by praising it further. Nearby is the Church of Santa Prassede, which possesses the column, brought from Jerusalem in 1223, after the sixth crusade, on which Christ is said to have leaned when he was scourged.

Near this church, on the Esquilino, is the basilica of Santa Maria Maggiore (St. Mary Major), so called because it is the largest church in Rome dedicated to the Virgin. It is also the oldest and one of the most magnificent of all Roman churches. In addition, it is an art museum, containing a Sistine Chapel less renowned than the one at St. Peter's but esteemed in its own right.

From the Middle Ages on, this church was regarded as one of the most important in the world and, as happened with all the important churches, it was adorned with the most beautiful reminders of pagan Rome. Some of the columns of its memorial chapel are taken from the Temple of Minerva.

On the Coelian Hill is a church that is better known to the world outside Rome. This is the basilica of San Giovanni in Laterano, named for the Lateran family, who lived here in the days of pre-Christian Rome. For a thousand years, the center of the Catholic Church was not the Vatican, but the Lateran Palace. It was not until the fourteenth century, when a pope of French origin moved to Avignon, in the south of France, that the Lateran lost its official position. A half century later, when the papacy was returned to Rome, the new pope decided to live in the Vatican.

The first basilica of the Lateran dates from the time of Constantine, but this was destroyed a century later. It has since undergone many complete or partial reconstructions, and is still the Cathedral of Rome.

It is noted for many works of art, and for its relics. In the Chapel of the Blessed Sacrament is a table supposed to be that of the Last Supper, while in this same chapel, serving less sacred purposes, are four columns of gilded bronze taken from the Temple of the Capitoline Jupiter. The Scala Santa, or Sacred Staircase, which stands before the Lateran Palace, consists of twenty-eight marble steps, protected by a wooden covering. Pilgrims to Rome climb it on their knees on their way to the *Sancta Sanctorum*, the pope's chapel, for it is the staircase which Christ is said to have climbed on his way to face Pontius Pilate.

In the Lateran Square, on the north side of the church, stands the oldest and largest obelisk in Rome. Carved of red granite and covered with hieroglyphics, it stood originally before the Temple of the Sun at Heliopolis in Egypt, but the ancient Romans brought it to a new site in front of the Circo Massimo, and in 1588 it was removed to its present position.

Between the churches of Santa Maria Maggiore and St. John Lateran, but off to one side, is a large open space, the Square of Victor Emmanuel II. This is a vast market, where fish and fowl are sold, along with vegetables, fruits, leather goods, and all sorts of odds and ends. As in so

Inside of railroad station showing the old wall at left

many places in Rome, cats abound, drawn here by the fragrance of the fish.

Off to the northeast we come to the main railroad station of Rome, Stazione Termini, begun under Mussolini, and completed after World War II. Parts of the very old wall of Servius Tullius, one of the early kings of Rome, are built into the very modern station. Beyond this is the large Piazza dei Cinquecento (Square of the

Outside of railroad station

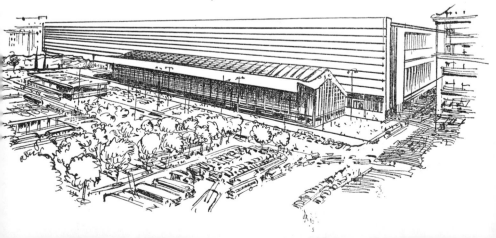

Inside of Opera Theatre

Five Hundred). In the same open area is the Piazza della Repubblica, formerly the Piazza dell'Esedra, and still known to most people by its old name. In ancient Greece an *exedra* was an outdoor area where it was possible to sit and converse. The chairs and tables of outdoor cafés line much of the square's circumference, and in the center is the well-known Fontana delle Naiadi (Naiads) which dates from the beginning of the present century.

The entire area is alive with pedestrians and traffic. Nearby are not only bus and subway terminals, but airline offices, restaurants, shops, churches, and theatres. The Opera Theatre is in one direction, the Ministry of Defense in a second, the Planetarium in a third. Other government offices, such as the Ministries of Agriculture and of Finance, are in the same area. But in our fourth direction—to the east of Piazza dell'Esedra—are the Baths of Diocletian, which, for the visitor, dwarfs the rest.

For the ordinary ancient Roman citizen, these famous Baths were the height of luxury. For a nominal fee, he could come here to bathe, get a rubdown by slaves, eat, drink, see his friends, converse with girl friends, watch popular entertainment or, if he had loftier tastes, listen to poetry or philosophy, take a nap after his exertions, bathe again, and so on all day. It was difficult to get work done, but that seemed unimportant, as there were slaves to do whatever needed doing. All the same, someone had to supervise the slaves, and someone else had to get himself killed or wounded defending the Empire, and as the people who did these dirty jobs became more and more envious of the slothful, happy Romans, they also tended to take their work much less seriously.

The growing luxury of Roman life—naturally, it was even more luxurious for the rich than for the ordinary citizen—is one of the causes to which the downfall of the Roman Empire is attributed. Whatever its importance in

Outside of Opera Theatre

Baths of Diocletian

this respect, the degeneration of the Roman character that accompanied the continual use of these baths impressed the early Christians. Perhaps the endless idling in the baths was a symptom rather than a cause of the real trouble, but in any case the conclusion was clear: bathing led to moral downfall. For more than a thousand years, dirtiness was next to godliness, and it was not until the past century that the opposite was considered true.

Nowadays no one is ruined by bathing in the Baths of Diocletian. They house the Museo Nazionale Romano delle Terme di Diocleziano (the National Roman Museum of the Baths of Diocletian), known more familiarly as the Museo delle Terme. Among its illustrious sculpture is the statue of Venus of Cyrene. Venus was the goddess of love and of fertility as well; therefore her statue was set up in many ancient Roman gardens. It is for this reason that so many Venuses are now to be found in museums all over the world, especially in Rome.

The Museo delle Terme also has The Girl of Anzio, a lovely statue found at Anzio, some thirty miles southeast of Rome. Americans will remember Anzio as the scene of a landing during World War II, and of a brave and costly fight put up by American soldiers to protect the beach from German troops.

Next door to the Museo delle Terme are statues of a less permanent cast, in a wax museum that offers an amusing contrast to the museum of marble.

A short distance from Piazza dell'Esedra is the Piazza San Bernardo, with its Fontana dell'Acqua Felice, literally Fountain of the Happy Water. The fountain was named for the Brother Felix who became Pope Sixtus V, but its waters actually recall unhappy memories of Prospero Bresciano, the sculptor of the statue in the fountain. He hoped to create a Moses that would rival Michelangelo's (see next page). When the statue was unveiled, the Romans broke into such derisive laughter that the

Michelangelo's Moses

Bresciano's Moses

miserable sculptor is said to have thrown himself into the Tiber.

With the exception of an occasional church or piece of sculpture, the entire area around Esedra seems so modern that it is difficult to think of it as the base of a gang of medieval robbers. At one time it contained about a hundred and forty towers from which the noble outlaws harried the city and the surrounding countryside. Eventually the robbers were killed off or merged into the general population, and the towers were torn down.

Piazza dell'Esedra is only about an eighth of a mile away from Via Venti Settembre (Twentieth of September Street), named to commemorate the day in 1870 when Victor Emmanuel's troops entered Rome and made it a part of the new kingdom of Italy. The street soon changes its name, as we go southwest, to Via del Quirinale. The building called the Quirinale is, naturally, on top of the

Quirinal Hill. It was created in 1574 by many of the best architects of the time, and became the summer residence of the popes, until Rome was lost to them in 1870. Now it is the home of presidents of the Italian Republic.

Government buildings line the Via del Quirinale on the right as we continue southwest to Quirinal Square, from which we can get a beautiful view of St. Peter's Basilica across the river. The buildings on the left side of the street are fortunately interrupted by gardens. One, belonging to a private group devoted to heliotherapy, or sun treatment, reminds us of the literal worship of the Sun by the Romans of two thousand years ago. Other gardens are public, and offer the visitor, as well as the Romans, charming places in which to relax.

If we turn downhill along Via delle Quattro Fontane (Street of the Four Fountains), we soon find ourselves outside the one-time Barberini Palace, which was built in the seventeenth century with stone taken, like that of so many other palaces, from the Colosseum. The build-

The changing of the guard at the Quirinale

ing is now the National Gallery, and houses many paintings, including a number of modern ones.

At the bottom of the hill we turn right into Barberini Square, which contains the Fountain of the Triton, another famous work of Bernini's. Now the square is an island surrounded by busy traffic and large buildings, but in Bernini's day there were trees and grassy hills around it, and the effect was entirely different. In the square, carriages wait for tourists, the drivers dozing with the horse reins in their hands.

If we skirt Barberini Square and continue in the same direction as the Street of the Four Fountains, we find ourselves on Via Sistina, which leads once more to the church of Santissima Trinità dei Monti, at the head of the Spanish Steps. But if we turn right off Barberini Square, we shall be on Via Vittorio Veneto, which leads up toward the Villa Borghese. (See also page 21.)

To some visitors, but to very few Romans, Via Veneto is the center of Roman life. It is a street of night clubs and outdoor cafés, of a small number of elegant shops, of tourist company offices, and of the luxurious Excelsior Hotel, where wealthy visitors stay. At the tables sit actors and actresses, directors, writers, and other the-

Via Vittorio Veneto

atrical and film people, as well as those who would like to associate with them. Here people come to display themselves and to see their competitors on display.

The worldly idlers of Via Veneto can find their rebuke on this same street if they wish, although nothing is further from the minds of most of them. Under the church of Santa Maria della Concezione (St. Mary of the Immaculate Conception) is a cemetery whose walls are ornamented with skulls and bones of monks of many generations. For those who like to draw grim morals, this is the proper place.

Also on the Via Veneto is the American Embassy, bustling with activity. Tourists from the United States tend to gravitate toward the Embassy, a symbol of home.

In this section of the city many extremes lie close together: ancient ruins, centuries-old churches, and modern night clubs; places to pray for heavenly salvation and places for worldly pleasure. This too is Rome, known through the ages for the strength of her religious feeling, and for the luxury and decadence of her people's lives.

The American Embassy

v.

THE OTHER SIDE OF THE TIBER

We may cross the Tiber at any of a number of bridges, to view sights sublime, grim, comic, and ridiculous, mixed in varying proportions. The Ponte Sublicio is at the same spot in the river where Horatius stood alone, in a poem familiar to generations of school children, and held the bridge against an invading army of Etruscans. The modern bridge leads to the Portese Gate. And around the corner from it, coming to life on Sunday mornings only, is a vast "flea market," about a mile long, where just about everything may be bought, including complete motorcycles, spare parts for cars and radios, tables, chairs, paintings, ornaments, jewelry, shoes, clothes, antiques, and "archaeological finds."

The "archaeological finds" are likely to be fakes for, if the Italian government cannot stop unauthorized digging, it can often prevent unauthorized buying and selling of what is found, and sales in the "flea market" are not authorized. But antiques that are a mere century or two old are likely to be genuine, as it is hardly worthwhile to fake objects that are so common. A tourist who

The flea market where bargains can sometimes be found

does not mind lugging an old candlestick holder or wooden statuette across the Atlantic may purchase genuine bargains—sometimes.

A short distance upstream from the Ponte Sublicio is the Isola Tiberina (Isle of the Tiber), connected by bridges to both banks. The island was once dedicated to Aesculapius, the Greek god of healing and, in a sense still is, as it houses a hospital. It faces the Teatro Marcello and the Jewish Sinagoga of Rome, both of them on the left bank.

Farther up the Tiber is the Ponte Sant'Angelo (the Bridge of the Holy Angel) whose stone angels were carved by Bernini and his assistants. The bridge leads directly to the Castel Sant'Angelo, a grim and impressive edifice whose existence led to the Vatican's replacing the Lateran as the center of the Catholic world. When the popes returned to Rome from Avignon in France, in the fourteenth century, they were well aware of the dangers of life in a city that had been pillaged by Gauls, Goths, Visigoths, Saracens, and supposedly friendly Christian kings and emperors as well. The Castel Sant'Angelo was the nearest thing to an impregnable fortress that the city had, and the Vatican was so short a distance away that an underground passage could be built between it and the castle. This passage was used frequently in the next few centuries and, on occasion, when danger was particularly threatening, the pope would make his home in the castle itself.

The Castel Sant'Angelo was originally built as a tomb for the pagan Emperor Hadrian. In the third century

Isola Tiberina

A.D., the Emperor Aurelian, concerned with defending the city against invaders, not only built his famous wall around Rome, but converted the tomb into a fortress. The divine visitor who gave the castle its new name was the Archangel Michael, who, toward the end of the sixth century, appeared to Pope Gregory the Great in a vision in which he sheathed his sword to announce the end of a plague that had devastated Rome as effectively as any invader. A statue of Michael now stands on top of the tower, looking as if he had just alighted.

Almost everything is gone that once characterized the building as a tomb. Once there were hanging gardens and great statues of Hadrian, but these have disappeared, along with the ashes of the Emperor. Some of the marble was used to make the tomb of Gregory XIII, and the lid of Hadrian's tomb is now supposed to be a font in San Pietro's. But most of the statues were broken into a num-

Castel Sant' Angelo and

ber of pieces and then were smashed completely by being hurled as missiles against the attacking Goths.

Pope Alexander VI, better known by his family name of Borgia, had apartments built for him in the castle, and constructed a dungeon where prisoners were tortured and then executed. It is said that no one ever emerged from this dungeon alive, but Benvenuto Cellini, goldsmith, engraver, murderer, and writer of a sensational autobiography, managed to

Archangel Michael at the top of Castel Sant' Angelo

Ponte Sant' Angelo

escape and tell about it. Both the apartments and the dungeon can be viewed by visitors, although the latter is not recommended to people suffering from claustrophobia. The entire castle has now been converted into a museum, and on display are paintings, weapons, and armor of the Middle Ages, as well as heaps of white stone cannon balls, ready for use in the ancient cannon.

Castel Sant'Angelo also figures in musical and dramatic history as the setting for the tragic ending of *Tosca*.

From the Castel Sant'Angelo, the broad Via delle Conciliazione (Street of the Reconciliation) leads to Piazza di San Pietro. The square and the great basilica, to which it provides a sort of architectural preface, are not actually part of Rome or Italy. They belong to Città del Vaticano (Vatican City), an independent state of 108 acres (about

one-sixth of a square mile) under the rule of the pope. Ever since a 1929 agreement with the Italian government, then under Mussolini, this tiny area has had its own laws, its own little army, its group of craftsmen and merchants, its own bank, newspaper, and radio broadcasting system, and even its own postal system. Its population varies, but is usually more than a thousand.

About twenty-five acres are occupied by the Basilica di San Pietro and by the group of buildings known as the Vatican Palace.

St. Peter's Square owes its greatness to Bernini, who planned the magnificent colonnades that adorn the sides, and designed ninety-six giant statues of saints and martyrs to top the great columns. Because of Bernini's skill, and because of the two fountains that cool the square on hot

The Pope blessing a crowd from his balcony

days, the area does not seem too large or unpleasantly empty. But on occasions when the pope speaks from his balcony, an estimated three hundred thousand people can be crowded into it.

St. Peter's Basilica, the largest church in the world, stands on the site of an earlier church erected in 324 A.D., the time of the Emperor Constantine, over a cemetery in which the body of St. Peter was said to be buried. The area had been previously occupied by Nero's Circus, of which only the obelisk now remains. This has been moved to the center of the square.

The old San Pietro was torn down by order of Pope Nicholas V, who began the building of the new church in 1450. This occupied a dozen of the greatest architects for more than a century and a half, among them Bramante, Raphael, Antonio Sangallo, and Michelangelo. The Basilica, though not completed, was finally consecrated in 1626, 176 years after it was begun, by Urban VIII, the Barberini Pope.

Construction of the main building and additions to it continued actively over another century and a half, and has gone on, to some extent, up to the present. As a result, the church does not have the architectural unity that the work of a single builder would have given it, and some critics have found fault with it for this reason. The average person is likely to be too overawed to think of this lack of unity. Only from the air can one see most of the structure at one time, and from this vantage point the dome and the square produce an overpowering effect.

St. Peter's is filled with treasures collected over the centuries. One column is believed to be from the temple of Jerusalem, and has great religious value because Christ is said to have leaned upon it. Additional columns were taken from Hadrian's Villa, of the first century A.D. In the Treasury is a collection of relics and precious objects dating back to such different periods as the Crucifixion and the reign of Charlemagne. On top of the bell tower is a clock from the ninth century, and other monuments are from years as recent as 1928 and 1949.

Among the most celebrated masterpieces are the Pietà of Michelangelo, completed when the sculptor was about twenty-four years old. Covering the tomb of St. Peter is Bernini's *baldacchino*, or canopy, made of bronze taken from the portico of the Pantheon, by order of Urban VIII.

This, and other acts of vandalism by the Barberini family, led the Romans to say that what the barbarians had not done, in the way of pillaging the monuments of antiquity, the Barberini had done. St. Peter's contains many highly ornamented chapels, altars, and tombs, as well as such other distinguished works by Bernini as the chair of St. Peter, the tomb of Urban VIII, and the tomb of Alexander VII.

If St. Peter's is difficult to grasp as a unit, the Vatican is impossible. But the Vatican was not meant to be a unit. It includes many palaces, chapels, galleries, and courts of different heights, built during the past seven and a half centuries. Paintings, statues, tapestries, and other works of art are so numerous that on any one day the visitor

The double spiral staircase leading to the Vatican's picture gallery

cannot hope to see more than a small fraction of those open to him. More than two hundred staircases link the floors in different sections of the Vatican, and as the corridors seem endless and confusing, a map is very helpful. An impressive double spiral staircase of marble and bronze, built in 1932, leads to the *Pinacoteca* (picture gallery). But there is also an elevator.

Perhaps the most famous single section in the entire Vatican is the Cappella Sistina (the Sistine Chapel), built for Pope Sixtus IV between 1473 and 1484. It is an oblong building used for conclaves. When a pope dies, the College of Cardinals meets, sleeps, and eats here until a new pope is chosen. The ceiling of the vault, painted by Michelangelo when he was a young man, represents the Creation of the World and of Man, the Fall of Man, and a prophecy of his Redemption. It includes many scenes from the Old Testament. In one of his sonnets, Michelangelo has left a vivid description of the tortures he suffered in the four years during which he worked seventy feet above the floor, with his head thrown back and his paintbrush raised to the ceiling. There is general agreement among other artists that they would spend an entire lifetime enduring such torture if they could create such masterpieces.

Michelangelo also designed the red, yellow, and blue uniforms still worn by the Swiss Guards who act as the police and army of the small state. (See next page.)

The Sistine Choir, renowned for its singing, figures in one of the most celebrated incidents in the history of music. No other singers had access to the *Miserere* of

Gregorio Allegri, a musical setting of the fifty-first psalm. Between performances the music used by the singers was kept under lock and key, and no copies were permitted to be made without authorization from the pope, under penalty of excommunication. During Easter Week of 1770, the composer Wolfgang Amadeus Mozart, then fourteen years old, heard a single performance—and wrote down the complicated music from memory, returning later to hear it again in order to correct a few minor errors. All Rome resounded with the news of the young man's feat, and even the pope, who had thereby lost exclusive control of the music, was pleased at this evidence of genius. Mozart was not excommunicated. Instead, he was made a Knight of a Papal Order.

At the same time that Michelangelo was painting the ceiling of the Sistine Chapel, his great contemporary, Ra-

The Swiss Guards of Vatican City

phael, was working on a series of paintings, mostly allegorical, that filled four rooms of the Vatican, among them the unsurpassed *School of Athens*, which portrays a number of well-known philosophers.

Other works of Raphael, along with paintings by Leonardo da Vinci, Titian, (Tiziano) Fra Lippo Lippi, and many other distinguished artists are in the Vatican's *Pinacoteca*. The seventy-seven original paintings of this collection were among those stolen by Napoleon in Rome and taken to France. Upon the downfall of the French Emperor, the British insisted that any that could be found should be returned to their owners. Returned they were, not to their original owners, but to Pius VII, who kept them at the Vatican in trust for the people of Rome. Since then the collection has grown very large, by more orthodox methods.

Among the noted pieces of sculpture in the vast collection of the Vatican are two ancient works now in the courtyard of the Belvedere. ("Belvedere" means "beautiful view," and the name is applied to any building that is built for the purpose of affording one.) The Laocoön illustrates a scene from Virgil's *Aeneid*, in which Laocoön, the priest of Apollo, and his two sons are strangled by serpents. The other statue, of Apollo himself, is known the world over as Apollo Belvedere.

Just north of Vatican City is the Piazza del Risorgimento (Square of the Revival), which refers to the movement for political unity in nineteenth-century Italy. This square is surrounded by a large, bustling, middle-class residential and shopping section.

About a mile southeast of Vatican City, extending along the Tiber from the Ponte Garibaldi to the Portese Gate, is the Trastevere (Across-the-Tiber) section. The poorest part of the city, it has existed for centuries with little change. Here lived the Romans who did not make history, but suffered while it was being made, usually at their expense. Many of them became soldiers, were killed or wounded, and received minor rewards when they were victorious. Only later, as the Empire grew rich, did they enjoy the luxuries of the baths, while their places in the army were taken by barbarian mercenaries, hired to fight the barbarians who threatened the empire from without.

Many of the streets of the Trastevere are narrow, winding, and picturesquely dirty. The cobblestones underfoot often date back to ancient and medieval Rome, and faucets in the streets still supply some of the houses with water. There are some ruins here—those of the Aurelian wall, for example—and there are several churches, especially Santa Maria in Trastevere, which are worth visiting. The main attraction of this section, however, is the picture it gives of the ordinary ancient Roman's way of life. (See picture, page 20.)

In addition, the Trastevere section contains a number of important buildings, among them Ministero Pubblica Istruzione (Ministry of Public Instruction) and the Palazzo Corsini, home of Accademia Nazionale dei Lincei (National Academy of the Lynxes).

Along the western side of the Trastevere section is the Janiculum, the hill named for Janus, the two-faced god. The Janiculum is the hill on which Lars Porsena camped with his army before being stopped by Horatius at the bridge. Five centuries later, Cleopatra stayed in a villa on the Janiculum when she visited Rome. Now the hill is noted for the beautiful homes on it, and for its memorials to Giuseppe Garibaldi. Not far from the statue of Garibaldi is one of his wife, Anita, who fought alongside him until she died of hunger and exhaustion.

Near the Queen of Heaven Prison (Carcere Regina Coeli) and the statue of Anita Garibaldi is a lighthouse with a flashing beacon. Hardly needed for ships, it may serve some purpose in guiding incoming planes.

From the top of the Janiculum, near the statue of Garibaldi, one can obtain a splendid view of the city, from Castel Sant'Angelo in the north to Piazza Navona, the Pantheon, the Capitoline, the Colosseum, the Palatine, Santa Sabina on the Aventine, and parts of the Coelian Hill. Many of the hills and squares look quite different when seen from the other side of the Tiber. Surpassing the god, Janus, who had only two faces, Rome has many aspects—some quite unexpected.

VI.

THE COMMUNITY OF ROME

*The Rome we have been visiting is, with few ex-*ceptions, the old city which the Emperor Aurelian tried to protect from the barbarians with his wall. If we have occasionally strayed beyond the wall, into Vatican City, for example, we have imitated the Romans themselves, for in the long run the wall was effective neither in keeping the Romans in nor the barbarians out.

This old Rome was divided into administrative districts called *rioni* even during the time of Augustus. The number of *rioni* and their boundary lines have changed with the centuries, but the name has been retained. The nine square miles of the ancient city are now divided into twenty-two *rioni*. Radiating irregularly outward from the center are the *quartieri*, or quarters, which are newer, although they too have their share of ruins. Beyond them are the *suburbi*, and beyond these the *Campagna*, or low-lying countryside that surrounds the city proper. The part of the countryside that extends sixteen or seventeen miles to the Tyrrhenian Sea at Ostia is part of the *Comune*, or Community, of Rome. The city administration governs the entire *comune*.

The administration is headed by a Mayor and a City Council of eighty members who are elected every four years. The Mayor is the chief executive, and presides over the meetings of an advisory board of fourteen members chosen, along with four alternates, from the City Council. The Council enacts city ordinances, while the advisory board sees to it that they are carried out. In an emergency, the board can act for the Council.

Rome has a city police force, a provincial force, for it is the capital of the province of Latium, and federal police as well. The fire department is controlled by the federal government.

The public school system begins with the Scuola Materna, or Maternal School, for children of kindergarten age, where, evidently, they are still mothered. At six, children must go to Elementary School, where they stay for five years. Here the young student learns to read and write, and then, at a relatively early age, although he continues with his general education, he may also begin to learn a trade. He can continue learning a trade in the intermediate school or go on with his study of the humanities and classics. The *ginnasio* and *liceo* are roughly equivalent to high school plus two years of college, and beyond them is the University.

In addition to the public schools, there are many parochial schools operated by various Catholic religious orders, all under control of the Ministry of Education.

The student who prefers to stay in Rome can go to the University of Rome, which was founded in 1303 by Pope Boniface VIII. The first college of the University was actually built in the sixteenth century near the Pantheon, and others eventually followed in the rest of the city. The present institution was opened in 1936 in Città Universitaria (University City), which is a little east of Stazione Termini and is near the Policlinico (Polyclinic Hospital).

The University, which is coeducational and has an enrollment of more than forty thousand, gives courses in a great variety of subjects, including literature, law, the physical sciences, architecture, biology, mathematics, medicine, and engineering. Tuition is low and so are the salaries of most of the teachers.

Rome has a number of academies and institutes devoted to the arts and sciences. The Accademia di San Luca is said to be the oldest academy of fine arts in all of Europe and America, while the Accademia Nazionale

University City

di Santa Cecilia and the Accademia Filarmonica Romana are important in the world of music. There are institutes of letters, medicine, and history, to say nothing of institutes for such prosaic, though important, subjects as agriculture. The Accademia Nazionale dei Lincei, which is near the Trastevere section on the right bank of the Tiber, has played a prominent role in the history of science. In ancient days, the lynx was credited with sight sharp enough to penetrate wood and stone. Scientists, such as Galileo, who joined the Academy of Lynxes, could boast of seeing into mysteries that were hidden from ordinary men. Nowadays, the Academy is not purely scientific, and has a large section devoted to the humanities.

Rome has, for three centuries and a half, been an important musical center, early composers such as Palestrina having worked here. Open-air productions of opera are given during the summer in the Baths of Caracalla, which

Concert at the Baths of Caracalla

are about three-quarters of a mile south of the Colosseum. It was in these great ruins that Shelley wrote his poem *Prometheus Unbound*. The amphitheatre is too large for perfect acoustics, but the spectacle on stage is magnificent, and reminds one of the lavish productions that dazzled royal courts in the early days of opera. There is, of course, the Opera House in the center of Rome which is open for the winter and spring, and the Rome Philharmonic Orchestra has its own season and hall. The Basilica di Massenzio is an impressive setting for symphonic concerts presented under the stars in the pleasant summer evenings. There are several other concert halls, notable among them being the Accademia di Santa Cecilia.

The auditorium of the Academy of Saint Cecilia has had a peculiar history. In order to modernize it, the directors ripped out old chairs, replaced torn upholstery with new material, and repaired the walls—only to find that they had ruined the hall's acoustical qualities. Many kinds of music no longer sounded right, and engineers were unable to restore the original acoustics, until someone had the idea of undoing all the repairs. The new chairs were replaced by old ones, the new upholstery either torn to make it old or replaced by as much of the old as could be found, and the walls restored to their previously damaged state, and Santa Cecilia became again one of the best concert halls in the world.

Rome has a number of theatres and movie houses which play at the same time that most Romans relax over their evening meal. Just as in the United States, the theatre-goer must either rush his meal or postpone it in order to attend. Theatre performances usually start at 9:15 P.M.; movies begin their final showing three quarters of an hour later.

There are a dozen or so restaurants that serve outstanding food in an unusual atmosphere, but even in most of the ordinary restaurants the food is good, and served in a variety of Italian styles, from Tuscan and Sardinian to Roman. You may wish to dine in a place that has historical associations—the Basilica Ulpia, for instance, in the ruins of Trajan's Basilica, or the Pancrazio, in the ruins of a building in which Caesar was assassinated. Or for a quick meal you may prefer a Tavola Calda, which may give you a choice of self-service or service by a waiter. There are one or two well-known American restaurants and bars in the center of Rome, and other restaurants that serve foreign foods. There are not many of these foreign restaurants, because the visitor is generally interested in tasting Italian foods, and the average Roman prefers them.

Everything in Rome is measured in the metric system. The standard weight is the *chilo*, which is about two and a quarter pounds. The standard measure of volume is the *litro*, somewhat more than a quart.

Rome offers the visitor food for the mind as well as the body. There are many libraries, the Accademia dei Lincei naturally having a collection of scientific books and journals, the Accademia di Santa Cecilia a collection of and about music, and so on. The Vatican has a famous library on religion and philosophy. Libraries are maintained by government departments, various institutions, and groups interested in special studies. Many of these

113

The Vatican library

Villa Medici

libraries are open to the public; others to scholars upon request.

Foreign organizations also share in the life of Rome. The French Academy of Art, which dates back to 1666, is housed in the old Villa Medici, where Galileo was held a prisoner by the Inquisition while awaiting trial. The Villa was acquired by Napoleon and used to provide studios for French artists. The American Academy in Rome, founded in 1894, is a comparative newcomer, and offers fellowships to architects, sculptors, painters, and scholars. There are also a British Academy, an American School of Classical Studies, and others.

There is a good-sized, fairly permanent foreign population as well. Rome is a world capital, and thousands of foreigners work for their governments here. Representatives of various business firms, movie people, students of all subjects from music and art to medicine, and families that enjoy its climate and tempo of life swell this number. Although there is no single foreign residential area, many Americans live in the Parioli district, because it is attrac-

The Parioli district

tive, and because it has an English-speaking school.

Almost one and a half square miles of public parks, villas, and gardens lie within the city, in addition to the numerous private parks. The public parks and gardens are administered by the Community of Rome not only in Rome itself but at Lido di Roma (also called Lido di Ostia), and Ostia, for instance. A twenty-five-hundred acre park at Castel Fusano, near Ostia, is also owned by the Community; a thousand acres are open to the public.

Rome was an open city for almost a year during World War II; that is, it was declared undefended and therefore was supposed to be left unattacked. Nevertheless it was bombed from time to time, occasionally by mistake. The aim of the bombers was bad, and the Vatican was among the places hit. Several thousand people were killed and many homes destroyed. After the war the housing short-age was so severe that thousands of people lived in caves.

Necessity forced the Community of Rome to start a housing program, and to begin public planning. New houses and new buildings of all kinds were built, and more are still needed, along with more roads to take care of the ever swelling flood of traffic. A second airport has already been built to take care of the growing number of travelers who come by air. The Romans are determined, however, that new buildings and roads shall not interfere with the preservation of the historical and architectural glories of the past. While this determination makes planning even more difficult than it is in an American city, it ensures that Rome will continue to be a city in which past and present are inextricably mingled.

OUTSIDE THE WALLS

The Rome that lies outside the walls of Aurelian is interesting in itself, and is also a convenient starting point for visits to nearby places. The *Campagna*, or countryside, around Rome contains many places that are worth seeing. A ride along the Old Appian Way to the south, for instance, takes the visitor past old tombs and ruins, with here and there the modern villa of a movie star or producer.

The Old Appian Way also leads to the Catacombs of St. Callixtus (Callisto), perhaps the most famous catacombs of all. This entire area was full of pagan tombs, and was taken over by the Christians of Rome only later. It was especially venerated because the bodies of Saints Peter and Paul were brought here after their executions. It should be noted that the catacombs were not a purely Roman institution, for they have been found in Naples, Sicily, and elsewhere, nor were they entirely Christian, for Rome had Jewish catacombs as well.

A modern burial ground, which brings bitter memories to the Romans who lived through World War II, is the

Fosse Ardeatine, the Ardeatine Ditches. In 1944, to avenge thirty-two German soldiers killed by the Italian Resistance, the Germans rounded up more than ten times that number of Romans, shot them, and dumped the bodies into a pit near a row of caves. A shrine and a cemetery now mark the caves.

More than a mile from the Porta San Paolo along the Via Ostiense, or Ostian Road, is the church of San Paolo Fuori le Mura (St. Paul Outside the Walls). About the same distance south from there are a street, an abbey, a church, and a sports stadium, all known by the name of Tre Fontane (Three Fountains). The fountains are said to date from the time when St. Paul was beheaded. His head is supposed to have bounced three times, producing a gush of water each time it struck the ground.

Beyond the Via delle Tre Fontane is the Esposizione Universale Romana (Universal Roman Exposition) so consistently referred to as EUR that even most maps do not give its full name. This is a group of impressive buildings in spacious surroundings, the construction of which was begun during the time of Mussolini for an Exposition

Esposizione Universale Romana (EUR)

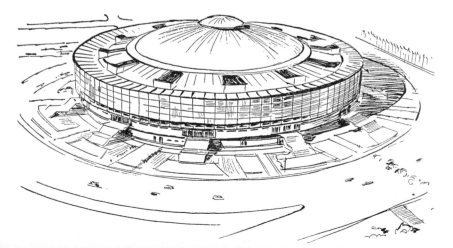

Foro Italico

planned for 1942 and never held. The buildings are now used for business purposes and for international meetings, and are surrounded by residences of the wealthy.

The late dictator's heavy taste in art and architecture are revealed here and in some of the enormously muscled statues in what was once the Foro Mussolini in the northwestern part of the city, intended to rival the forums of Julius Caesar and other empire builders. After Mussolini's downfall this became the Foro Italico, and an Olympic stadium, sports fields, tennis courts, and swimming pools were built here for the Olympic games of 1960. They are still put to good use, for the Italian interest in sports continues to grow.

The Parioli district is in the northern part of the city. Its broad avenues, large parks, and modern buildings form part of a residential area that was once highly fashionable. Later on, still newer buildings were constructed in other districts and lured away some of the wealthier residents, but the Parioli district remains a pleasant and comfortable place in which to live. Residences for the embassy staffs of a number of governments, including that of the United States, are there.

About six and a half miles off to the southeast, in the direction of the famous Roman aqueducts, is Cinecittà (Cinema City) the home of busy movie studios. Like studios the world over, they are closed to the general public. In the same general direction, between thirteen and twenty miles from the city are the Castelli Romani, literally Roman Castles or Manors, but actually the name of a region where villages existed even before the founding of Rome. Castles, villas, and churches are scattered among the hills and woodlands once sacred to the Roman gods. In this same area lies Frascati, which is famous for its wines, and Castel Gandolfo, an ancient town that contains the summer home of the popes. The Papal Villa is not quite three and a half centuries old.

Even the bus trip southwest to the airport at Fiumicino takes the traveler past the ruins of ancient Ostia, where the baths, the old Palace of Hadrian, and a number of temples are well worth looking at. A large theatre is still used to present occasional plays there, including those of the old Roman dramatist, Plautus. Near the ancient city, the ruins of a two-thousand-year-old Jewish synagogue and a well-kept cemetery with old Greek and Roman inscriptions will fascinate the archaeologically minded visitor.

In the opposite direction from Ostia, twenty miles from Rome, lies Tivoli, another great attraction for visi-

Ancient Ostia

Modern Ostia

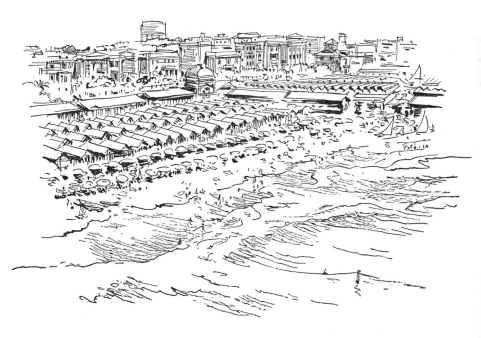

tors. On the way from Rome to Tivoli are the ruins of Hadrian's Villa. One is reminded here of Coleridge's poem,

> *"In Xanadu did Kubla Khan*
> *A stately pleasure dome decree. . . ."*

for the Villa is a pleasure town, decreed by Hadrian. About three miles in diameter, this Villa contained so many buildings—theatres, libraries, living quarters, even swimming pools—that the Emperor himself must have found it difficult to keep track of everything he had. Swans now glide along the great pool where Hadrian and his parasites enjoyed bathing, and sheep graze among the ruins.

Many of the statues and other works of art had been collected—often by force, as an emperor collects—in Greece, Italy, Egypt, and Asia, but only a small propor-

Villa d'Este

The fountains in the gardens at Villa d'Este

tion of the original collection now remains. Hadrian was
followed by a number of kings, other emperors, and popes
whose passion for art was as great as his own, and many
of the masterpieces on which his eyes feasted are now to be
found in Roman churches or French museums. The Mari-
time Theatre, built on an island in one of the pools, still
remains to delight the visitor, chiefly because an island is
difficult to take away.

At Tivoli itself is the Villa d'Este, a masterpiece surrounded by grass, trees, and water. More than a hundred
fountains break into jets and plumes of water in gardens

laid out on the side of a steep hill. The Villa was ordered built in 1550 by the Cardinal d'Este, son of the famous or infamous Lucrezia Borgia (almost everyone in the family was reputed to be a poisoner, and the more energetic members used swords and daggers to commit murder as well). The Villa d'Este is a cool and beautiful oasis in the hot countryside.

The saying that all roads lead to Rome, like many a geometrical theorem, is true in reverse: all roads lead away from Rome, and from this former capital of a great Empire one can travel easily to all towns and cities of Italy, and to other countries as well. It is not necessary to toss a coin into the Fountain of Trevi to ensure your return to Rome. The allure of the city will be sufficient to draw you back, with its turbulent history and its tranquillity, its vitality and its laziness in the summer sun, its art and beauty so fascinatingly mingled with ugliness, its mixture of old and new, of the most solemnly religious and the most vulgarly profane, matched nowhere else on earth.

ACKNOWLEDGMENTS

We are grateful to Signora Matizia Maroni of the Fondazione "Ernesta Besso" for her warmth, kindness and encouragement. She gave most generously of her time and knowledge, read much of the manuscript, and offered many suggestions. If any errors survive in the text, they are ours alone.

We also wish to thank Signor Luigi Coppe, of EPT (Ente Provinciale Turismo), Signora Trapani, Signora Salomone, and Signor Pasquale M. Scala of ENIT (Ente Nazionale Industrie Turistiche) and Signor Siegfried Maovaz of CIT (Compagnia Italiana Turismo), all of whom we found cooperative and thoughtful far beyond the call of duty.

We appreciate the cooperation of the United States Information Service, of RAI (Italian Broadcasting System) and of academies, museums, and officials too numerous to name here.

Words cannot express our feelings to our hosts, Professore and Signora Gianfranco Mazzuoli, whose friendship and warm hospitality made us feel at home, and helped us to understand and share in the Roman way of life.

And, finally, we wish to express our affection and thanks to the people of Rome, whose pride in their city, and friendly, lively spirit we have tried to capture.

D.S./J.S.

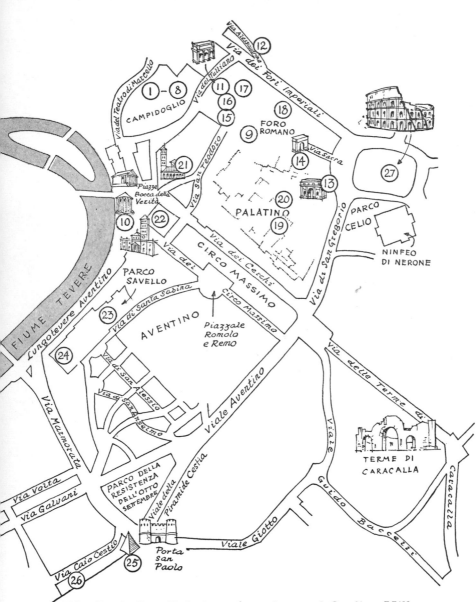

The Capitoline, Palatine, Aventine, and Coelian Hills

1. Rupe Tarpeia (Tarpeian Rock)
2. Santa Maria d'Aracoeli
3. Museo Capitolino
4. Palazzo dei Conservatori
5. Palazzo Senatorio
6. Marco Aurelio statue
7. Dioscuri (Castor & Pollux statues)
8. She-wolf cave
9. Casa delle Vestali (House of the Vestal Virgins)
10. Tempio di Vesta (Temple of Vesta)
11. Arco di Settimio Severo (Arch of Septimus Severus)
12. Foro di Augusto (Forum of Augustus)
13. Arco di Constantino
14. Arco di Tito
15. Miliarium Aureum (Golden Milestone)
16. Umbilicus Urbis (Navel of the City)
17. Lapis Niger
18. Basilica di Massenzio (sometimes called Constantino)
19. Casa di Livia (sometimes called Augustus)
20. Casino Farnese
21. San Giorgio in Velabro
22. Santa Maria in Cosmedin
23. Santa Sabina
24. Piazza dei Cavalieri di Malta (Square of Knights of Malta)
25. Piramide Caio Cestia
26. Cimitero Protestante
27. Colosseo

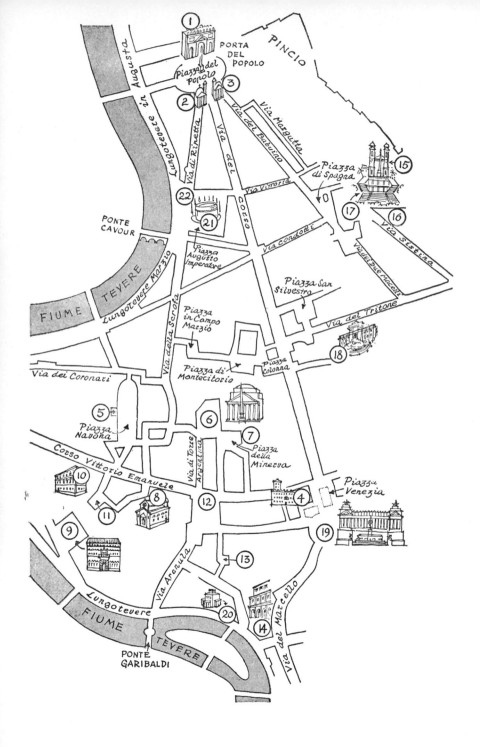

1. Santa Maria del Popolo
2. Santa Maria dei Miracoli
3. Santa Maria di Montesanto
4. Palazzo Venezia
5. Sant'Agnese in Agone
6. Pantheon (Sancta Maria ad Martyres)
7. Santa Maria Sopra Minerva
8. Sant'Andrea della Valle
9. Palazzo Farnese
10. Cancelleria
11. Piazza Campo di Fiori
12. Largo di Torre Argentina
13. Piazza Mattei
14. Teatro Marcello
15. Santissima Trinità dei Monti
16. Keats-Shelley Memorial
17. Scala di Spagna
18. Fontana di Trevi
19. Monumento a Vittorio Emanuele II
20. Sinagoga
21. Mausoleo di Augusto
22. Ara Pacis

Starting from Porta del Popolo: to Piazza Venezia; to Theatre of Marcellus; to Victor Emmanuel Monument

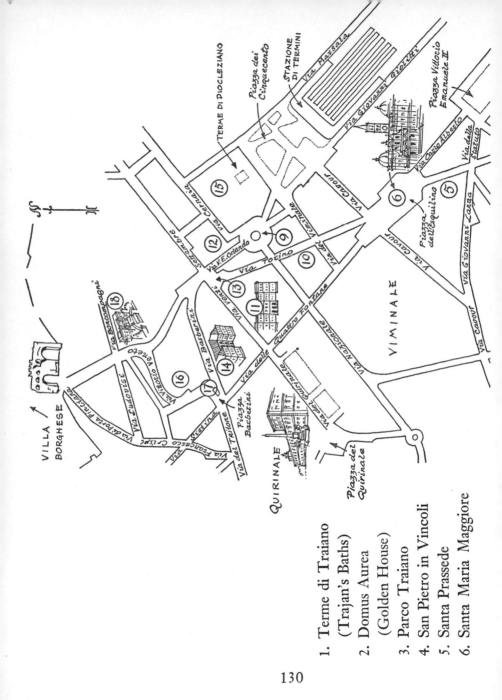

1. Terme di Traiano
   (Trajan's Baths)
2. Domus Aurea
   (Golden House)
3. Parco Traiano
4. San Pietro in Vincoli
5. Santa Prassede
6. Santa Maria Maggiore

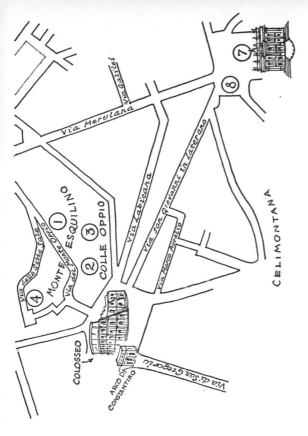

The Esquiline, Coelian, Quirinal, and Viminal Hills

7. San Giovanni in Laterano
   and Sancta Sanctorum
8. Piazza San Giovanni
   in Laterano
9. Piazza dell'Esedra (now
   Piazza della Repubblica)
10. Teatro dell'Opera
11. Ministero del Difesa
    Esercito (Ministry of
    Defense)
12. Planetario
13. Piazza San Bernardo
14. Palazzo Barberini
    (National Gallery of Art)
15. Museo Nazionale Romano
16. Santa Maria della
    Concezione
17. Fontana del Tritone
18. American Embassy

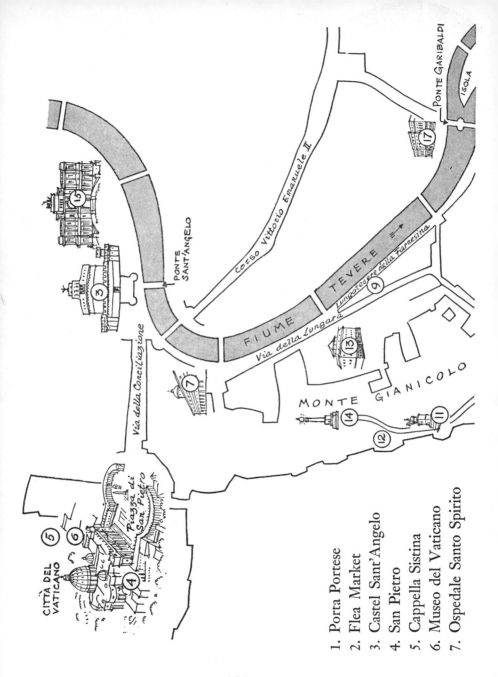

1. Porta Portese
2. Flea Market
3. Castel Sant'Angelo
4. San Pietro
5. Cappella Sistina
6. Museo del Vaticano
7. Ospedale Santo Spirito

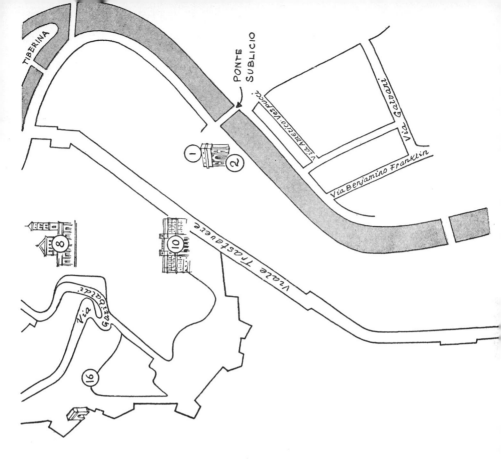

8. Santa Maria in Trastevere
9. Accademia Nazionale dei Lincei
10. Ministero della Pubblica Istruzione
11. Giuseppe Garibaldi (statue)
12. Anita Garibaldi (statue)
13. Carcere Regina Coeli (Queen of Heaven Prison)
14. Faro del Gianicolo (Lighthouse)
15. Palazzo di Giustizia
16. American Academy
17. Ministero Grazia e Giustizia

Across the Tiber

133

PRONUNCIATION GUIDE

All of the Italian words in the text are listed below, by chapter, as they first appear. They are not repeated.

Italian is derived from Latin. Many English words are also formed from Latin roots; therefore the reader may be able to understand a number of Italian words because of their similarity to corresponding English words. Spoken Italian is quite different, however, and this guide attempts to offer only a reasonable approximation of the sound of the words.

CHAPTER I

Fiume Tevere	Fee-*you*-may *Tay*-vay-ray
Campidoglio	Kahm-pee-*doh*-lyoh
Romolo	*Roh*-moh-loh
Remo	*Ray*-moh
Campo Marzio	*Kahm*-poh *Mar*-tsee-oh
Tempio Ninfa Egeria	*Taym*-pee-oh *Neen*-fah Ay-jay-ree-ah
Numa Pompilio	*Noo*-mah Pawm-*pee*-lee-yoh
Via Appia Antica	*Vee*-ah *Ahp*-pee-ah Ahn-*tee*-kah
Scipione	Shee-pee-*oh*-nay
Domine, Quo Vadis? (Latin)	*Doh*-mee-nay Quoh *Vah*-dees
Foro Romano	*Foh*-roh Roh-*mah*-noh
Colosseo	Koh-lohs-*say*-oh
Giulio Cesare	Jee-*oo*-lee-oh *Chay*-zah-ray
di Augusto	dee Ah-oo-*goos*-toh
Mausoleo d'Adriano	Mah-oo-zoh-*lay*-oh d'Ah-dree-*ah*-noh
Terme di Diocleziano	*Tayr*-may dee Dee-oh-klay-tzee-*ah*-noh
Caracalla	Kah-rah-*kahl*-lah
Basilica di San Pietro	Bah-*zee*-lee-kah dee Sahn Pee-*ay*-troh

134

Fontana di Trevi	Fawn-*tah*-nah dee *Tray*-vee
Catacombe	Kah-tah-*kohm*-bay
Monte Mario	*Mawn*-tay *Mah*-ree-oh
Istituto Astronomico	Ee-stee-*too*-toh Ah-stroh-*noh*-mee-koh
Otterino Respighi	Oht-tay-*ree*-noh Ray-*spee*-gee
Veneto	*Vay*-nay-toh
Largo di Torre Argentina	*Lahr*-goh dee *Tohr*-ray Ahr-jayn-*tee*-nah
Garibaldi	Gah-ree-*bahl*-dee
Piazzale	Pee-ahtz-*tzah*-lay
Ponte	*Pawn*-tay
Cavour	Kah-*voor*
Piazza Vittorio Emanuele	Pee-*ahtz*-tzah Veet-*toh*-ree-oh Ee-mahn-oo-*ay*-lay
Cola di Rienzo	*Koh*-lah dee Ree-*ayn*-tzoh
Giorgio	Jee-*awr*-jee-oh
Bolivar	Boh-lee-*vahr*
Americo Vespucci	Ah-may-*ree*-koh Vay-*spoo*-chee
Ferdinando Gregorovius	Fayr-dee-*nahn*-doh Gray-goh-*roh*-vee-oos
Gianicolo	Jee-ah-*nee*-koh-loh
Parco della Rimembranza	*Pahr*-koh *dayl*-lah Ree-maym-*brahn*-tzah
delle Scienze	*dayl*-lay Shee-*ayn*-tzay
Fermi	*Fayr*-mee
Alberto	Ahl-*bayr*-toh
Galvani	Gahl-*vah*-nee
Volta	*Vohl*-tah
Galilei	Gah-lee-*lay*-ee
Euclide	Ay-oo-*klee*-day
Pitagora	Pee-*tah*-goh-rah
Archimede	Ahr-kee-*may*-day
Socrate	*Soh*-krah-tay
Viale Da Vinci	Vee-*ah*-lay Dah *Veen*-chee
Lungotevere Michelangelo	Loon-goh-*tay*-vay-ray Mee-kayl-*ahn*-jay-loh
Eleanora Duse	Ay-lay-ah-*noh*-rah *Doo*-zay
Tommaso Salvini	Tohm-*mah*-soh Sahl-*vee*-nee

Giuseppe Verdi	Jee-oo-*sayp*-pee *Vayr*-dee
Gioacchino Rossini	Jee-oh-ahk-*kee*-noh Raws-*see*-nee
Paisiello	Pah-ee-zee-*ayl*-loh
Giordano Bruno	Jee-awr-*dah*-noh *Broo*-noh
Acquasanta	Ah-quah-*sahn*-tah
Acqua Acetosa	*Ah*-quah Ah-chay-*toh*-zah
Ostia	*Aws*-tee-ah
Lido di Roma	*Lee*-doh dee *Roh*-mah
Aniene	Ah-nee-*ay*-nay
Cinecittà	Chee-nay-cheet-*tah*
Parioli	Pah-ree-*oh*-lee
Tavola Calda	*Tah*-voh-lah *Kahl*-dah
Trattoria	Traht-toh-*ree*-ah
Ristorante	Ree-stoh-*rahn*-tay
Villa Borghese	*Veel*-lah Bawr-*gay*-zay
Galoppatoio	Gah-lohp-pah-*toy*-oh
Caligula	Kah-*lee*-goo-lah
Corso	*Kawr*-soh
Porta del Popolo	*Pawr*-tah dayl *Poh*-poh-loh
Palazzo Venezia	Pah-*latz*-tzoh Vay-*nay*-tzee-ah
Assisi	Ahs-*see*-see
Paolina	Pah-oh-*lee*-nah
Milvio	*Meel*-vee-oh
Flaminia	Flah-*mee*-nee-ah
Raffaello	Rahf-fah-*ayl*-loh

CHAPTER II

Capitolino	Kah-pee-toh-*lee*-noh
Juno Moneta (Latin)	Jee-*ooh*-noh Moh-*nay*-tah
Rupe Tarpeia	*Roo*-pay Tahr-*pay*-ah
Spurius Tarpeius (Latin)	*Spoo*-ree-oos Tahr-*pay*-oos
Palatino	Pah-lah-*tee*-noh
Aventino	Ah-vayn-*tee*-noh
Livy	*Lee*-vee
Santa Maria d'Aracoeli	*Sahn*-tah Mah-*ree*-ah d'Ah-rah-*chay*-lee
Buonarroti	Boo-oh-nahr-*roh*-tee

Museo	Moo-*zay*-oh
dei Conservatori	*day*-ee Kohn-sayr-vah-*toh*-ree
Senatorio	Say-nah-*toh*-ree-oh
Tabulario	Tah-boo-*lah*-ree-oh
Sindaco	*Seen*-dah-koh
Dioscuri	Dee-*oh*-skoo-ree
Sacra	*Sahk*-rah
Curia	*Koo*-ree-ah
Vaccino	Vah-*chee*-noh
Lazio	*Lah*-tzee-oh
Casa delle Vestali	*Kah*-zah *day*-lay
	Vay-*stah*-lee
Foca	*Foh*-kah
Settimio Severo	Sayt-*tee*-mee-oh Say-*vay*-roh
Tito	*Tee*-toh
Massenzio	Mahs-*sayn*-tzee-oh
Tullianum (Latin)	Tool-lee-*ahn*-oom
Miliarium Aureum (Latin)	Mee-lee-*ah*-ree-oom
	Ah-oo-*ray*-oom
Umbilicus Urbis (Latin)	Oom-*bee*-lee-koos *Oor*-bees
Lapis Niger (Latin)	*Lah*-pees *Nee*-jayr
Giulia	Jee-*oo*-lee-ah
Tiberio	Tee-*bay*-ree-oh
Domiziano	Doh-mee-tzee-*ahn*-oh
Eliogabalo	Ay-lee-oh- *gah*-bah-loh
Frangipani	Frahn-jee-*pah*-nee
Casino Farnese	Kah-*see*-noh Fahr-*nay*-zay
Velabro	Vay-*lah*-broh
Circo Massimo	*Cheer*-koh *Mahs*-see-moh
Savello	Sah-*vayl*-loh
Sabina	Sah-*bee*-nah
Cavalieri di Malta	Kah-vah-lee-*ay*-ree dee
	Mahl-tah
Porta San Paolo	*Pawr*-tah Sahn Pah-*oh*-loh
Piramide Caio Cestio	Pee-*rah*-mee-day *Kah*-ee-oh
	Chays-tee-oh
Cimitero Protestante	Chee-mee-*tay*-roh Proh-tay-
	stahn-tay
Cosmedin	*Kawz*-may-deen
Bocca della Verità	*Bawk*-kah *dayl*-lah
	Vay-ree-*tah*

Caravaggio	Kah-rah-*vahj*-jee-oh
Gian Lorenzo Bernini	Jee-*ahn* Loh-*rayn*-zo Bayr-*nee*-nee
Lucrezia Borgia	Loo-*kray*-tzee-ah *Bawr*-jee-ah
Pincio	*Peen*-chee-oh
Margutta	Mahr-*goot*-tah
Miracoli	Mee-*rah*-koh-lee
Montesanto	Mawn-tay-*sahn*-toh
Lata	*Lah*-tah
Umberto Primo	Oom-*bayr*-toh *Pree*-moh
Benito Mussolini	*Bay*-nee-toh Moos-soh-*lee*-nee
Ripetta	Ree-*payt*-tah
Imperatore	**Eem-pay-rah-*toh*-ray**
Ara Pacis (Latin)	*Ah*-rah *Pah*-chees
Navona	Nah-*voh*-nah
Agnese in Agone	Ah-*nyay*-zay een Ah-*goh*-nay
Pamphili	Pahm-*fee*-lee
Moro	*Moh*-roh
Coronari	Koh-roh-*nah*-ree
Circlo Agonale	*Cheer*-kloh Ah-goh-*nah*-lay
Pantheon	*Pahn*-tay-ohn
Sancta Maria ad Martyres (Latin)	*Sahnk*-tah Mah-*ree*-ah ahd *Mahr*-tee-rayz
Sopra Minerva	*Soh*-prah Mee-*nayr*-vah
Sant'Andrea della Valle	Sahnt-Ahn-*dray*-ah *dayl*-lah *Vahl*-lay
Cancelleria	Kahn-chayl-lay-*ree*-ah
Fiori	Fee-*oh*-ree
Teatro	Tay-*aht*-roh
Ministero Grazia e Giustizia	Mee-nee-*stay*-roh *Grah*-tzee-ah ay Jee-oo-*stee*-tzee-ah
Mattei	Maht-*tay*
Tartarughe	Tahr-tah-*roo*-gay
Colonna	Kaw-*lawn*-nah
Marcello	Mahr-*chayl*-loh
Babuino	Bah-boo-*ee*-noh
Vittoria	Veet-*toh*-ree-ah
Cecilia	Chay-*chee*-lee-ah
Condotti	Kawn-*dawt*-tee

138

Scala di Spagna	*Skah*-lah dee *Spah*-nyah
Santissima Trinità dei Monti	Sahn-*tees*-see-mah Tree-nee-*tah* day-ee *Mawn*-tee
Silvestro	Seel-*vays*-troh
Tre Vie	Tray *Vee*-ay
Vittoriano	Veet-toh-ree-*ah*-noh

CHAPTER IV

Gregorio	Gray-*goh*-ree-oh
Celio	*Chay*-lee-oh
Nazionale	Nah-tzee-oh-*nah*-lay
Quirinale	Quee-ree-*nah*-lay
Viminale	Vee-mee-*nah*-lay
Esquilino	Ays-quee-*lee*-noh
Colle Oppio	*Kawl*-lay *Awp*-pee-oh
Domus Aurea (Latin)	*Doh*-moos *Ah*-oo-ray-ah
Traiano	Trah-ee-*ah*-noh
Vincoli	*Veen*-koh-lee
Prassede	Prahs-*say*-day
Maggiore	Mahj-jee-*aw*-ray
Giovanni in Laterano	Jee-oh-*vahn*-nee een Lah-tay-*rah*-noh
Sanctorum (Latin)	Sahnk-*toh*-room
Stazione Termini	Stah-tzee-*oh*-nay *Tayr*-mee-nee
Servius Tullius (Latin)	*Sayr*-vee-oos *Tool*-lee-oos
Cinquecento	Cheen-quay-*chayn*-toh
Repubblica	Ray-*poob*-blee-kah
Esedra	Ay-*zay*-drah
Naiadi	*Nah*-ee-ah-dee
Bernardo	Bayr-*nahr*-doh
Felice	Fay-*lee*-chay
Prospero Bresciano	*Proh*-spay-roh Bray-shee-*ah*-noh
Venti Settembre	*Vayn*-tee Sayt-*taym*-bray
Quattro Fontane	*Quaht*-troh Fawn-*tah*-nay
Barberini	Bahr-bay-*ree*-nee
Sistina	Sees-*tee*-nah
Concezione	Kawn-chay-tzee-*oh*-nay

CHAPTER V

Sublicio	Soo-*blee*-chee-oh
Portese	Pawr-*tay*-zay
Isola Tiberina	*Ee*-zoh-lah Tee-bayr-*ee*-nah
Sinagoga	See-nah-*goh*-gah
Castel Sant'Angelo	Kahs-*tayl* Sahn-*tahn*-jay-loh
Benvenuto Cellini	Bayn-vay-*noo*-toh Chayl-*lee*-nee
Conciliazione	Kawn-chee-lee-ah-tzee-*oh*-nay
Città del Vaticano	Cheet-*tah* dayl Vah-tee-*kahn*-oh
Bramante	Brah-*mahn*-tay
Antonio Sangallo	Ahn-*toh*-nee-oh Sahn-*gahl*-loh
Pietà	Pee-ay-*tah*
Baldacchino	Bahl-dahk-*kee*-noh
Pinacoteca	Pee-nah-koh-*tay*-kah
Cappella	Kahp-*payl*-lah
Miserere	Mee-zayr-*ayr*-ay
Gregorio Allegri	Gray-*goh*-ree-oh Ahl-*lay*-gree
Leonardo da Vinci	Lay-oh-*nahr*-doh dah *Veen*-chee
Tiziano	Tee-tzee-*ah*-noh
Fra Lippo Lippi	Frah *Leep*-poh *Leep*-pee
Belvedere	Bayl-vay-*day*-ray
Risorgimento	Ree-sawr-jee-*mayn*-toh
Trastevere	Trahs-*tay*-vay-ray
Pubblica Istruzione	*Poob*-blee-kah Ees-troo-tzee-*oh*-nay
Corsini	Kawr-*see*-nee
Accademia Nazionale dei Lincei	Ahk-kah-*day*-mee-ah Nah-tzee-oh-*nah*-lay *day*-ee *Leen*-chay-ee
Carcere Regina Coeli	*Kahr*-chay-ray Ray-*jee*-nah *Chay*-lee

140

CHAPTER VI

Rioni	Ree-*oh*-nee
Quartieri	Quahr-tee-*ay*-ree
Suburbi	Soo-*boor*-bee
Campagna	Kahm-*pah*-nyah
Comune	Kaw-*moo*-nay
Scuola Materna	Skoo-*oh*-lah Mah-*tayr*-nah
Ginnnasio	Jeen-*nah*-zee-oh
Liceo	Lee-*chay*-oh
Universitaria	Oo-nee-vayr-see-*tah*-ree-ah
Policlinico	Paw-lee-*klee*-nee-koh
Luca	*Loo*-kah
Filarmonica Romana	Feel-ahr-*moh*-nee-kah Roh-*mah*-nah
Palestrina	Pah-lay-*stree*-nah
Ulpia	*Ool*-pee-ah
Pancrazio	Pahn-*krah*-tzee-oh
Chilo	*Kee*-loh
Litro	*Lee*-troh
Medici	*May*-dee-chee
Fusano	Foo-*zahn*-oh

CHAPTER VII

Callisto	Kahl-*lees*-toh
Fosse Ardeatine	*Faws*-say Ahr-day-ah-*tee*-nay
Ostiense	Aws-tee-*ayn*-zay
Fuori le Mura	Foo-*oh*-ree lay *Moo*-rah
Esposizione Universale	Ay-spoh-zee-tzee-*oh*-nay Oo-nee-vayr-*sah*-lay
Italico	Ee-*tah*-lee-koh
Castelli Romani	Kah-*stayl*-lee Roh-*mah*-nee
Frascati	Frah-*skah*-tee
Gandolfo	Gahn-*dohl*-foh
Fiumicino	Fee-oo-mee-*chee*-noh
Tivoli	*Tee*-voh-lee
Villa d'Este	*Veel*-lah *d'Ay*-stay

141

INDEX

Bernini, Gian Lorenzo, works of: 57, 62, 65, 90, 94; in St. Peter's Square and Basilica, 99, 101, 102; biography of, 62–63; father of, 70

Bernini, Pietro, work of, 70

Black Stone, 47

Blessed Sacrament, Chapel of, 82

Bocca della Verità, 54–55

Bolivar Square, 21–22

Bonaparte, Napoleon, 33; and Cancelleria, 66; and Vatican paintings, 105; and Villa Medici, 115

Boniface VIII, Pope, 110

Borghese family, 33

Borghese, Villa, 90; features of, 30; history of, 31, 33

Borgia, Cesare, 57

Borgia, Lucrezia, story of, 57; son of, 124

Bramante, and St. Peter's, 101

Brazilian Embassy, 62

Bresciano, Prospero, Moses statue of, 87–88

British Academy, 115

Broad Street, 59

Bruno, Via Giordano, 22

Buonarroti, Michelangelo, *see* Michelangelo

Byron, George Gordon, 33, 70

Caesar, Julius, street named for, 13; story of, 47–48; structures begun by, 47–48; plans of, for Rome, 56; defeat of Pompey by, 65; and Venus, 77; building in which he was assassinated, 113

Caesars, city of, 10

Caligula, Emperor, 30, 50

Callisto, *see* St. Callixtus

Campagna, 108, 117

Campidoglio, 11, 50, 73

Campidoglio, Piazza del, 39

Campo dei Fiori, Piazza, 66

Campo Marzio, *see* Martian Field

Campo Vaccino, 44

Campus Martius, *see* Martian Field

Cancelleria, 65–66

Capitol, derivation of, 37; *see also* Campidoglio

Capitol Square, description of, 39; *see also* Capitolino *and* Campidoglio

Capitoline Museum, statues in, 39

Capitolino, 77; purposes, significance, and character of, 35–37; and legend, 35–36; buildings and statues on, 39–42, 82; view from, 43, 45

Cappella Sistina, *see* Sistine Chapel

Caracalla, Baths of, 13; concerts at, 111–112

Caravaggio, Michelangelo da, works of, 57

Carcere Regina Coeli, 107

Carthage, empire of, 13

Castel Gandolfo, 120

Castelli Romani, 120

Castor, statute and story of, 40

Castor and Pollux, Temple of, 44

Catacombe, 15, 64, 117

Cathedral of Rome, 82

Cavalieri di Malta, Garden of, 52

Cavour, Benso di, 66

Cavour, Piazza, 66–67

Cavour Street, 21

Celio, *see* Coelian Hill

Cellini, Benvenuto, escape of, from Castel Sant'Angelo, 97–98

Cestius, Caius, Pyramid of, 54

Charles VIII, of France, 61

Cimitero Protestante, 54

Cinecittà, 25, 120

Cinquecento, Piazza dei, 83–84

Circlo Agonale, 63

Circo Massimo, 52, 82

Citadel, on Capitolino, 36, 37

Città del Vaticano, *see* Vatican City

Città Universitaria, *see* University City

City Hall, 39

City of Canals, Venice as, 10

City of Cats, Rome as, 10

City of Fountains, Rome as, 10

City of Illusion, Rome as, 14

City of the Dead, under Rome, 14–15

Cleopatra, visit of, to Rome, 107

Coelian Hill, 76; church on, 81

Cola di Rienzo, Street and Square, 21

Colle Oppio, *see* Oppian Hill

Colonna, Piazza, location of, 67

Colosseum, building and uses of, 13, 79–80; stone from, for other buildings, 80, 89

Commodus, Emperor, and Colosseum, 80

Conciliazione, Via delle, 98

Condotti, Via, shops on, 69

Constantine, Emperor, Basilica of, 13, 49; and Marcus Aurelius statute, 40; Arch dedicated to, 45; and St. Peter's Basilica, 100

Conservatori, Palazzo dei, statues in, 39

Corsini, Palazzo, 106

Corso, Via del, 59, 61; and horse races, 30–31

Curia, in Roman Forum, 44

Da Vinci, Leonardo, 105

Da Vinci, Viale Leonardo, 22

Diocletian, Baths of, 13; history of, 85–86

Dioscuri, *see* Castor and Pollux

Domine, Quo Vadis?, church, 13

Domitian, Emperor, 50, 61

Domus Aurea, *see* Golden House

Duse, Via Eleanora, 22

EUR, 118–119

Egeria, Temple of the Nymph, 11

Einstein, Via Alberto, 22

Eliogabalo, *see* Heliogabalus

Emanuele, Corso Vittorio II, church on, 65

Emanuele, Piazza Vittorio II, 21, 82–83

Emanuele, Vittorio II, monument to, and biography of, 70, 72, 73–74; and unification of Italy, 70, 72, 88

Emanuele, Vittorio III, and Fascists, 73

Esedra, Piazza dell', 84, 87; history of, 88

Esposizione Universale Romana, 118–119

Esquilino, 76, 77; Golden House on, 77; church on, 81

Este, Cardinal d', 124

147

Navona, Piazza, buildings, cafés, and fountains in, 61–62; ruins in, 63

Nazionale, Via, location of, 76

Nero, Emperor, legend about, 56–57; and burning of Rome, 57, 75; Golden House of, 77, 79; statue of, 77

Nero's Circus, original location of, 100

Nicholas V, Pope, and St. Peter's, 100

Numa Pompilius, 11

Octavius, *see* Augustus

Old Appian Way, *see* Appia Antica

Olympics, stadium for, 30, 119

Open City, 14

Opera Theatre, 84, 112

Oppian Hill, 77

Oppian Park, 79

Osier Hill, 76

Ostia, 24, 108; parks and gardens in, 116; ruins of, 120

Ostia, Lido di, 116

Ostiense, Via, 118

Paisiello, Via, 22

Palatino, and legend, 36; House of Romulus on, 37; archaeological finds on, 37; Forums on, 49; buildings on, 49, 51, 76

Palestrina, Giovanni, 111

Pamphili, Palazzo, 62

Pancrazio, 113

Pantheon, 63–64; bronze from, in St. Peter's, 101

Parioli district, homes in, 26, 115–116, 119–120

Paul, Saint, imprisonment of, 47; statue of, 67; burial place of, 117; legend about, 118; *see also* St. Paul *and* San Paolo

Peter, Saint, and church, 13; imprisonment of, 47; burial place and tomb of, 100, 101, 117; *see also* St. Peter *and* San Pietro

Phocas, statue to, 45

Pinacoteca, at Vatican, 103, 105

Pincio, 57

Pines of Rome, The, 16

Piramide Caio Cestia, 54

Pitagora, Piazza, 22

Pius VII, Pope, and Vatican paintings, 105

Planetarium, 84

Plautus, plays of, 120

Pollux, statue and story of, 40; temple of, 44

Pompey, temple built by, 65

popes, residences of, 81–82, 89, 94, 97, 120; chapel of, 82; as rulers of Vatican City, 99; and St. Peter's Square, 100

Popolo, Piazza del, 61; in ancient times, 57; in recent times, 57, 59

Popolo, Porta del, 33, 56; and horse races, 31

Portese Gate, 92, 106

presidents, residence of, 89

Prometheus Unbound, 112

Protestant Cemetery, 54

Pythagoras, *see* Pitagora

quartieri, 108

Quattro Fontane, Via delle, 89, 90

Queen of Heaven Prison, 107

Quirinal Hill, 89

149

also names; parks and gardens in, 26, 30, 31, 51, 52, 89, 116, 119, 123–124, *see also names;* population and size of, 16–17, 23; religion in, 9, 10, 15, 22–23, 31, 35, 44, 45, 80, 81–82, *see also names of churches;* restaurants in, 17, 21, 28, 30, 59, 62, 84, 90, 113, *see also names of;* sayings about, 9, 124; shops and shopping in, 28, 59, 63, 68, 69, 70, 74, 82, 90, 105; streets and street names in, 13, 20–23, *see also names of streets;* traffic in, 19–20, 25, 31, 54, 74, 84, 90

Rome Philharmonic Orchestra, 112

Romulus and Remus, legend about, 11, 36, 68

Romulus, founding of city by, 11, 36; Temple of, 11; and Capitolino, 35; House and wall of, 37; grave of, 47

Rossini, Gioacchino, 66

Rossini, Viale Gioacchino, 22

Rupe Tarpeia, 36

Sabines, Tarpeia and, 36

Sacra, Via, triumphal processions on, 43, 47

Sacred Staircase, 82

St. Callixtus, Catacombs of, 117

St. Paul Outside the Walls Church, 47, 118

St. Paul's Gate, 54

St. Peter's Basilica, 13; views of, 52, 89; Sistine Chapel of, 81, 103–104; lid of Hadrian's tomb in, 96; area occupied by, 99;

history of, 100–101; treasures in, 101–102

Salvini, Via Tommaso, 22

San Antonio's Day, 31

San Bernardo, Piazza, 87

San Giorgio in Velabro Church, 54

San Giovanni in Laterano, basilica of, 81–82; works of art in, 82

San Gregorio, Via di, 76

San Luca, Accademia di, 110

San Paolo, *see* St. Paul *and* Paul, Saint

San Paolo Fuori le Mura, 47, 118

San Paolo, Porta, 54

San Pietro, *see* St. Peter's *and* Peter, Saint

San Pietro in Vincoli Church, 81

San Pietro, Piazza di, 98; and Bernini, 99–100

San Silvestro, Piazza, bus terminal, post office, and shops on, 70

Sancta Maria ad Martyres Church, 64

Sancta Sanctorum, 82

Sangallo, Antonio, and St. Peter's Basilica, 101

Sant'Agnese in Agone Church, 62

Sant'Andrea della Valle Church, 65

Sant'Angelo, Castel, 94–98

Sant'Angelo, Ponte, 94

Santa Cecilia, Accademia Nazionale di, 69, 110–111; auditorium of, 112; library in, 113

Santa Maria d'Aracoeli Church, 39

151

Tosca, settings for scenes of, 65, 98

Trajan, Basilica of, restaurant in, 113

Trajan, Baths of, 79

Trastevere section, description of, 106

Tre Fontane, 118

Tre Vie, explanation of, 70

Trevi, Fontana di, 14, 70, 124

Triton, Fountain of, 90

Tullianum, remains of, and prisoners in, 45, 47

Tullius, Servius, old wall of, 83

Umberto I, Via, 59

Umbilicus Urbis, 47

Universal Roman Exposition, 118–119

University City, location of, 110

University of Rome, 110

Unknown Soldier of Italy, tomb of, 74

Urban VIII, Pope, 101, 102

Vatican, publishing done by, 25; and Catholic Church, 81–82, 94; buildings and treasures of, 102–105; library in, 113; bombing of, 116; *see also names of buildings and* Vatican City

Vatican City, location, area, property, and government of, 56, 66, 98–99; *see also* Vatican

Vatican Palace, area occupied by, 99

Velabro, 52

Veneto, Via Vittorio, buildings and life on, 17, 90–91

Venezia, Palazzo, 31, 59

Venezia, Piazza, 59, 61; and Victor Emmanuel Monument, 73–74

Venti Settembre, Via, 88

Venus, statues of, 86

Vercingetorix, as prisoner, 47

Verdi, Piazza Giuseppe, 22

Vespasian, Emperor, and Colosseum, 79

Vespucci, Via Americo, 22

Vesta, worship of, 45

Vestal Virgins, House of, 44–45

Vibenna, Coelius, 76

Viminale Hill, 76

Vinegary Water, Street of, 23

Virgil, *Aeneid* of, 105

Vittoria, Via, location of, and Academy on, 69

Vittorio Emanuele, *see* Emanuele, Vittorio

Volta, Via, 22

Washington, Giorgio, Avenue, 21

wax museum, 87

PRINTED IN U.S.A.